GENERATIONS *of* FAMILY FAVOURITES

Book Two

GENERATIONS

of

FAMILY FAVOURITES

Book Two

RJ WOODWARD

iUniverse, Inc.
Bloomington

Generations of Family Favourites Book Two

iUniverse books may be ordered through booksellers or by contacting:

iUniverse
1663 Liberty Drive
Bloomington, IN 47403
www.iuniverse.com
1-800-Authors (1-800-288-4677)

ISBN: 978-1-4620-1303-6 (pbk)
ISBN: 978-1-4620-1304-3 (ebk)

Printed in the United States of America

iUniverse rev. date: 05/11/2011

CONTENTS

Prologue

Every family has favourite recipes that have passed down through the generations. I have spent a good part of my life wishing someone in our family would take the time to compile some of their favourites.

As children we were encouraged to express ourselves through cooking. Many of these recipes have been tried, tested and loved by all. They have been expressed in a level that even the youngest reader can attempt their first creations without fear of failure.

Take this book and make it your recipe box, mark the recipes you love, add your own to the extra pages provided and encourage future generations to pass them on. A small wish but a great demand.

Our family is a circle of love and strength. With every birth and every union, the circle grows. Every joy shared adds more love. Every crisis faced together makes the circle stronger. Memories have been cherished as well as our recipes.

"The belly rules the mind."—Spanish Proverb
"If God had intended us to follow recipes,
He wouldn't have given us grandmothers."
—Linda Henley

RJ Woodward

*"Look to this day . . . . for yesterday is already a
dream and tomorrow is only a vision."*

*"A friend is someone who knows the song in your
heart, and can sing it back to you when you have
forgotten the words."*

<u>Author of</u>:

<u>Eyes Closed, Too Hear</u>—ISBN/SKU 9781450261975 soft cover
9781450261982 E-book

<u>Generations of Family Favourites</u>—ISBN/SKU
9781450290357 soft cover
9781450290364 E-book

Chapter One

Entrees

"At twenty we worry about what others think of us; at forty we don't care about what others think of us; at sixty we discover they haven't been thinking about us at all."

Homemad-e Tartar Sauce

1 cup mayonnaise
½ cup chopped dill pickles
1 teaspoon capers, chopped
2 teaspoons Dijon mustard
2 teaspoons chopped shallots
2 Tbsp chopped scallions
2 teaspoons lemon juice
6 drops Tabasco sauce or more to taste
Salt and pepper to taste

Mix all ingredients together in a bowl.
Makes about a cup and a half of tartar sauce.

Hint

Flip over your favorite plastic food storage container and check the recycling code number. If you spy a number 3 or 7, well, those containers should probably go to the craft room or garage to store buttons or screws rather than food.

~º ~º ~º ~º ~º ~º ~º ~º ~º ~º ~º ~º

Buffalo Wings

Wings: 2 pounds chicken wings (about 12 wings)
3 tablespoons butter, melted
4 tablespoons bottled hot pepper sauce
1 tablespoon paprika
½ teaspoon salt
½ teaspoon cayenne pepper
¼ teaspoon black pepper
Celery sticks (optional)
Blue cheese dip: ½ cup sour cream
½ cup crumbled blue cheese
½ cup mayonnaise
1 tablespoon white wine vinegar or white vinegar
1 clove garlic, minced

Wings: Cut off wing tips. Cut wings at the joint. Put chicken wing pieces in a plastic bag. Set aside.

Food safety note: when cutting raw chicken it is best to use a cutting board reserved just for cutting raw chicken. Wash thoroughly when finished. Do not let raw chicken juices come in contact with other food.

Create a marinade by stirring together the melted butter, hot pepper sauce, paprika, salt, cayenne pepper and black pepper. Pour all but 2 tablespoons of the marinade over the chicken pieces in the plastic bag. (Reserve marinade for coating after the pieces come out of the oven.) Seal bag and let marinate at room temperature for half an hour. When marinating is finished, drain marinade and discard bag.

Place wing pieces on the rack of a broiler pan. Broil 4-5 inches from the heat for about 10 minutes on each side, until chicken is tender and no longer pink. Remove from oven and baste with reserved marinade.

Serve with Blue Cheese Dip and celery sticks. Makes approximately 24 pieces (about 12 appetizer servings).

Blue cheese dip: Combine dip ingredients—sour cream, mayonnaise, blue cheese, vinegar, and garlic—in a blender or food processor. Blend or pulse until smooth. Cover and chill up to a week.

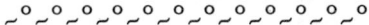

"Nobody can go back and start a new beginning, but anyone can start today and make a new ending."—Maria Robinson

English Muffin Pizzas

6 muffin halves
1 cup grated Mozzarella cheese, packed
1 tablespoon butter
1 medium onion, sliced thin
¾ cup diced ham pinch of chopped fresh sage
¼ teaspoon stone ground mustard
Optional: A few slices of fresh tomato

Preheat oven to 425 °F.

Melt butter in a medium skillet on medium high heat. Add the onions and cook until translucent, about 5 minutes. Add the diced ham, cook 5 minutes more. Mix in the sage and mustard. Remove from heat.

Put muffin halves, open side up on a sturdy baking pan. Distribute the cheese evenly, sprinkling over the muffin halves. Put the onion ham mixture on top of the cheese. If you want to use tomato slices, layer them between the cheese and onion mixture.

Bake @ 425°F for 8-9 minutes, until the muffins and toppings are nicely browned, but not burnt. Cut into quarters for appetizers or just leave whole for a meal or snack.

~°~°~°~°~°~°~°~°~°~°~°~°~°~°~°

Pâté (Pate) Maison

1 pound chicken livers
1 pound lean pork
1 pound mild Italian sausage meat
1 tablespoon chopped chives or scallions
1 tablespoon chopped parsley
1 tablespoon fresh coarsely ground pepper
½ teaspoon ground ginger
½ teaspoon cinnamon
1 teaspoon salt
2 tablespoon brandy
2 tablespoon dry sherry
10 slices bacon (uncooked)

Grind all the meat (except the bacon) through a meat grinder twice. Add remaining ingredients and mix well.

Line 9 x 5 x 3 inches loaf pan with bacon strips and pack in the mixture. Cover with bacon strips. Place pan in a water bath, a larger pan that is filled halfway up the sides of the inner pan with water. Bake @ 350°F for 2½ hours.

Remove from heat. Cover with aluminum foil. Place a weight such as a heavy brick on top while cooling. Best to cool overnight in the refrigerator. Slice and serve with bread or toast, lettuce and or tomatoes.

Yield: one large loaf.

°~°~°~°~°~°~°~°~°~°~°~°~°~°

Jet Swirl Pizza

1 (10 ounces) can refrigerated pizza crust dough
¼ pound Genoa salami, thinly sliced
¼ pound pepperoni sausage, sliced
¼ pound provolone cheese, sliced
½ cup shredded mozzarella cheese

Preheat oven to 350 °F (175 °C). Lightly grease a large baking sheet.

Roll pizza crust dough into an approximately 10 x 14 inch rectangle on the baking sheet. Layer with Genoa salami, pepperoni and provolone cheese. Sprinkle with mozzarella cheese to within ½ inch from edges of the dough. Roll jelly roll style. Seal the edge with a fork.

Bake in the preheated oven 25 minutes, or until golden brown. Slice into 1 inch pieces to serve.

°~°~°~°~°~°~°~°~°~°~°~°~°~°

"The key to change . . . is to let go of fear."—Rosanne Cash

The Best Cheese ball

2 (8 ounces) packages cream cheese, softened
¾ cup shredded Cheddar cheese
¼ cup shredded pepper jack cheese
½ green bell pepper, minced
1 jalapeno peppers, seeded and minced
1 teaspoon Worcestershire sauce
½ teaspoon garlic salt

In a medium bowl combine the cream cheese, Cheddar cheese, Monterey Jack cheese, green bell pepper, jalapeno pepper, Worcestershire sauce and garlic salt. Mix together and form mixture into a ball. Roll ball in cilantro and serve with your favorite crackers.

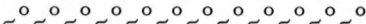

TIP:
Milk which is slightly turned or changed may be sweetened and rendered fit for use again by stirring in a little baking soda.

Party Sandwich Loaf loaf

unsliced sandwich bread softened butter
1 hardboiled egg, chopped
1 1/3 cups cooked shrimp, finely chopped
¼ cup celery, finely chopped
2 tablespoons lemon juice
¼ teaspoon salt dash of pepper
¼ cup mayonnaise
3 oz. cream cheese, softened
1 cup toasted pecans, finely chopped
1 can (8 3/4 ounces) crushed pineapple, well drained
8 slices bacon, crisply fried and crumbled

1 cup cooked chicken, finely chopped
¼ cup mayonnaise
1 tablespoon pimiento, finely chopped
¼ teaspoon salt
1/8 teaspoon pepper
2 packages (8 ounces each) cream cheese, softened ½ cup light cream
2-3 drops green food colouring, or enough to tint a delicate green

Shrimp Salad Filling:
1 hardboiled egg, chopped
1 1/3 cups cooked shrimp, finely chopped
1/4 cup celery, finely chopped
2 tablespoons lemon juice
¼ teaspoon salt dash of pepper
¼ cup mayonnaise

Cheese Pecan Filling:
3 ounces cream cheese, softened
1 cup toasted pecans, finely chopped
1 can (8 3/4 ounces) crushed pineapple, well drained

Chicken Bacon Filling:
8 slices bacon, crisply fried and crumbled
1 cup cooked chicken, finely chopped
¼ cup mayonnaise
1 tablespoon pimiento, finely chopped
¼ teaspoon salt
1/8 teaspoon pepper

Cream Cheese Frosting:
2 packages (8 ounces each) cream cheese, softened ½ cup light cream
2-3 drops green food coloring, or enough to tint a delicate green

RJ Woodward

Prepare fillings by mixing together all ingredients for each filling and for cream cheese frosting.

Trim the crusts from 1 loaf of unsliced sandwich bread. Cut loaf horizontally into 4 equal slices.

Spread one sides of 3 slices with softened butter.

Place 1 slice, buttered side up, on a serving plate. Spread evenly with shrimp salad filling. Top with the second bread slice and spread evenly with Cheese-Pecan filling. Top with third slice and spread evenly with Chicken Bacon filling. Top with remaining bread slice. Frost top and sides with Cream Cheese frosting.

Chill until frosting has set—about 30 minutes. Wrap loaf with a damp cloth and chill 2½ hours or overnight.

꙾ ꙾ ꙾ ꙾ ꙾ ꙾ ꙾ ꙾ ꙾ ꙾ ꙾ ꙾ ꙾

Sweet Potato Burritos

1 tablespoon vegetable oil
1 onion, chopped
4 cloves garlic, minced
6 cups canned kidney beans, drained
2 cups water
3 tablespoons chili powder
2 teaspoons ground cumin
4 teaspoons prepared mustard
1 pinch cayenne pepper, or to taste
3 tablespoons soy sauce
4 cups sweet potatoes, cooked and mashed
12 (10 inch) flour tortillas, warmed
8 ounces shredded Cheddar cheese

Preheat oven to 350 °F (175 °C).

Heat oil in a medium skillet, and sauté onion and garlic until soft. Stir in beans, and mash. Gradually stir in water, and heat until warm. Remove from heat, and stir in the chili powder, cumin, mustard, cayenne pepper and soy sauce.

Divide bean mixture and mashed sweet potatoes evenly between the warm flour tortillas. Top with cheese. Fold up tortillas burrito style, and place on a baking sheet.

Bake for 12 minutes in the preheated oven, and serve.

_°_°_°_°_°_°_°_°_°_°_°_°_°_°

Breaded, Fried, Softly Spiced Tofu

1 (16 ounces) package extra-firm tofu, drained and pressed
2 cups vegetable broth
3 tablespoons vegetable oil
½ cup all purpose flour
3 tablespoons nutritional yeast
1 teaspoon salt
½ teaspoon freshly ground black pepper
1 teaspoon sage
½ teaspoon cayenne pepper

Cut pressed tofu into ½ inch thick slices; then cut again into ½ inch wide sticks. Place tofu in a bowl, and pour broth over the top. Set aside to soak.

In a separate bowl, stir together flour, yeast, salt, pepper, sage, and cayenne.

Warm oil in a large skillet over medium-high heat.

Remove tofu sticks from broth, and squeeze most of the liquid from them. Roll sticks in breading. (You may have to roll sticks twice to end up with a fairly dry outer layer of breading.) Place tofu in hot oil; fry until crisp and browned on all sides. Add more oil if necessary.

_°_°_°_°_°_°_°_°_°_°_°_°_°_°

> *"You've achieved success in your field*
> *when you don't know whether what*
> *you're doing is work or play."*
> —*Warren Beatty*

Crispy Barbequed Tofu Slices

1 (16 ounces) package extra firm tofu
3 tablespoons olive oil
1 egg white
1 tablespoon barbeque sauce
1 cup all purpose flour
1 teaspoon salt
½ teaspoon pepper
1 cup barbeque sauce

Drain tofu, and slice into strips. Place in a plastic bag or container, and freeze overnight. This will give the tofu a meatier texture. Thaw tofu strips, and blot with paper towels to dry.

Heat olive oil in a large skillet over medium heat. In a small bowl, whisk together the egg white and 1 tablespoon of barbeque sauce. Combine the flour, salt, and pepper in a separate bowl. Dip the tofu slices into the egg mixture, then into the flour mixture, shaking off excess flour. Fry in the hot oil for about 1 minute on each side, until golden brown. Just fry enough at one time so they are not crowded. Remove from the oil to paper towels to drain and cool.

Preheat the oven's broiler. Brush tofu slices with additional barbeque sauce, and allow to marinate while the broiler heats up. Arrange them on a broiler pan, or wire rack set over a cookie sheet for best results.

Position the oven rack about 6 inches from the heat source. Broil for 5 minutes on each side, or until browned and crisp, watching closely so as not to burn them. Serve warm with the remaining barbeque sauce for dipping.

~°~°~°~°~°~°~°~°~°~°~°~°~°

Italian Appetizer—Bagna Cauda

An excellent garlic dip that is easy to make with a few ingredients. Serve warm with Italian bread, lettuce leaves, green pepper, celery, broccoli or cauliflower.

1½ cups extra virgin olive oil
4 tablespoons butter
4 cloves garlic, minced
2 tablespoons heavy cream freshly ground black pepper to taste

In a saucepan over medium heat, combine the olive oil and butter. Season with black pepper. Heat until butter melts, then add garlic. Cook until garlic has softened but not browned. Remove from heat, and stir in cream. Serve warm.

~°~°~°~°~°~°~°~°~°~°~°~°~°

Corned Beef Dip

1 (12 ounces) can canned corned beef
1 (1 ounce) envelope dry onion soup mix
1 (16 ounce) container sour cream

Mix all ingredients in a bowl, cover, and chill for 1 hour.

~°~°~°~°~°~°~°~°~°~°~°~°~°

"The doors we open and close each day decide the lives we live."—Flora Whittlemore

TIP:

Always grate nutmegs at the blossom end first.
To Test Nutmegs
Prick them with a pin; if good, the oil will instantly spread around the puncture.

<u>MY SPECIAL RECIPES</u>

Chapter Two

Breads and Buns

Tips
How To Make Bread Bowls

❧ *Start with a round loaf of crusty sourdough or French bread from a bakery or make your own.*

❧ *Use a serrated knife to slice off the top of the round crusty bread loaf.*

❧ *Cut or pull the soft center of the loaf away from the shell, leaving a 1-inch thickness of soft bread dough around the inside of the crust.*

❧ *Melt 1/4 cup butter or olive oil with 1 clove of pressed garlic and 1 tsp minced fresh parsley.*

❧ *Brush inside of bread bowl and dough side of lid with butter mixture.*

❧ *Bake in conventional or toaster oven at 400 °F. for 5 to 10 minutes until golden.*

❧ *Let cool.*

Tips:

* *Bake your own bread rounds or purchase them at the bakery.*
* *The top may be used as a lid or cut into dippers.*
* *Save the inside bread dough for croutons or bread crumbs.*
* *You may omit the butter, oil, and garlic, if you wish.*
* *Use bread bowls to serve soups, stews, chowders, dips, and spreads. Encourage eating of the bowl.*

Basic Needs:

* *Conventional or toaster oven.*
* *Round loaf of French, sourdough or other crusty bread.*
* *Butter, margarine, or olive oil.*
* *Garlic press.*
* *Garlic.*
* *Serrated knife.*
* *Fresh parsley.*

Tip:
<u>*How to Soften Butter Quickly*</u>

Just put the stick of butter between two large pieces of wax paper. Using a rolling pin, press down on the butter. Roll it out they way you would roll out a pie crust. When the butter is about 1/8-¼ inch thick, lift off the wax paper and peel away the butter (before it gets too soft to peel).

Softened butter, ready for beating.

> *"There is nothing wrong with change, if it is in the right direction."*
> *—Winston Churchill*

Green Chile Cornbread

1 cup + 2 tablespoons cornmeal
1 cup all purpose flour
1½ teaspoons salt
1 teaspoon baking soda
1 tablespoon baking powder
¼ cup sugar
½ cup (1 stick) softened unsalted butter
½ cup sour cream
2 eggs
1¾ cups milk
2 cups green chiles, roasted, chopped
1 cup corn (frozen is fine)
1 cup (4 ounces) cheddar or Monterey Jack cheese, grated

Preheat oven to 400°F. Grease 8 x 12 inches baking dish.

In a large bowl mix the cornmeal, flour, salt, baking powder and baking soda. In a separate bowl, beat the softened butter and sugar. Beat the sour cream and eggs to the butter sugar mixture. Add the milk and the dry ingredients, a third at a time and alternating wet/dry. Mix in the green chiles, corn, and shredded cheese. Pour mixture into prepared baking dish.

Bake for 35 minutes, until top is browned, the center springs back when pressed down, and a skewer inserted into the center comes out clean. Let cool almost completely before serving.

Makes about 12 serving pieces.

TIP:
A bowl containing two quarts of water, set in an oven when baking, will prevent pies, cakes, cookies, etc., from being scorched.

۔°۔°۔°۔°۔°۔°۔°۔°۔°۔°۔°۔°۔°۔°

Basic Sourdough Starter

2 cups all—purpose flour
3 tablespoons sugar
1 tablespoon (1 envelope) dry active yeast
½ teaspoon salt
2 cups warm water (105 °F, 40 °C)

In a 6 cup plastic container; combine all ingredients, beat with wooden or plastic spoon. Cover container, set in warm place free from drafts. Allow to ferment 2-3 days. Stir several times a day.

To use: remove starter needed for recipe. Refrigerate remaining starter in a plastic container that has an air vent or hole in it. Label container.

Replenish every 7-10 days by stirring in equal amounts of water and all purpose flour. After replenishing allow to stand at room temperature over night. Return to refrigerator. If a clear liquid forms on top, stir back into starter.

˷°˷°˷°˷°˷°˷°˷°˷°˷°˷°˷°˷°

Rye Bread

1½ cups warm water (105 °F, 40 °C)
1 tablespoon (1 envelope) dry active yeast
1 cup sourdough starter
3 tablespoons sugar
3 tablespoons butter or margarine, softened
2 teaspoons caraway seeds
2 teaspoons salt
3 cups rye flour
2-3 cups all purpose flour

Warm a large bowl. Pour water and yeast into warmed bowl. Set aside 5 minutes. Stir in sourdough starter, sugar, butter, caraway seeds, salt and rye flour, beat until blended. Turn onto lightly floured surface; knead dough 8-10 minutes or until smooth. Shape dough into a ball. Place in greased bowl, turning to grease all sides. Cover with cloth, let rise in warm draft free area for 1½ hours or until double in size. Punch down, shape into 2 loaves. Place in greased pans. Cover, let rise in warm draft free area 1-2 hours until double in size. Preheat oven 375 °F (190 °C). Bake 35-40 minutes or until golden brown. Remove from pans, cool.

 ̴° ̴° ̴° ̴° ̴° ̴° ̴° ̴° ̴° ̴° ̴° ̴° ̴°

Sourdough Hotcakes

At night: take sourdough starter from fridge.
Add: 1¾ cups flour
1 tablespoon sugar
1¼ cup warm water

Mix this and beat well
Let stand overnight covered with cloth.
Next day: take 1 cup and store in plastic container for next time. Do not store in metal container. You can also freeze this sourdough.
Add to remainder: 2 eggs
1 tablespoon sugar
Pinch salt
Beat until smooth. Add 1 heaping teaspoon baking soda dissolved in a little hot water. Cook in hot griddle.

Pumpernickel Bread

1 tablespoon (1 envelope) dry active yeast
½ cup warm water (105 °F, 40 °C)
1 cup sourdough starter
1 teaspoon salt
¼ cup molasses
2 tablespoons vegetable oil
1 tablespoon caraway seeds
1½ cups rye flour
1 cup whole-wheat flour
1-2 cups all purpose flour
Vegetables oil for tops of loaves

Sprinkle yeast over water. Set aside for 5 minutes. In a large bowl combine sourdough starter, softened yeast mixture, salt, molasses, oil and caraway seeds. Beat in rye flour and whole-wheat flour. Stir in enough all purpose flour to make a stiff dough. Turn out on a lightly floured surface. Knead 8-10 minutes or until smooth. Place in greased bowl, turning all sides in greases. Cover with cloth and set aside in warm draft free area. Let rise 1-2 hours or until double in size. Grease 9 x 5 inches loaf pan. Punch down dough; shape into loaf and place in pan. Cover with cloth and place in warm draft free area and allow to rise 1-2 hours or until ½ inch above rim of pan. Preheat oven to 350 °F (175 °C). Bake 50-60 minutes or until loaf sounds hollow. If loaf browns to fast cover with a tent of foil to prevent further browning. Remove from pan. Cool.

°~°~°~°~°~°~°~°~°~°~°~°~°~°

Cranberry Orange Muffins

1½ cups all purpose flour
2 teaspoons baking powder
½ teaspoon salt
¼ cup sugar
1 egg
½ cup sourdough starter
¾ cup orange juice
1/3 cup vegetable oil
1 tablespoon orange peel, grated
¾ cup canned whole cranberry sauce
½ cup chopped walnuts or pecans.

Grease 18 muffin cups or line with paper liners; set aside. Preheat oven to 400 °F (205 °C). In a large bowl, stir together flour, baking powder, salt and sugar; set aside. In a medium bowl, beat egg, stir in sourdough starter, orange juice, oil and peel. Add to flour mixture. Stir with a fork until dry ingredients are just moistened, fold in cranberry sauce and nuts. Fill prepared muffin cups 2/3 full. Bake 20-25 minutes or until tops are golden brown.

Red Pepper Corn Bread Muffins

1¼ cups (300 ml) cornmeal
1 cup (250 ml) all-purpose flour
¼ cup (50 ml) chopped fresh coriander or parsley
1½ teaspoons (7 ml) baking powder
½ teaspoon (2 ml) baking soda

1/4 teaspoon (1 ml) salt
2 eggs
1½ cups (375 ml) buttermilk
2 tablespoons (25 ml) butter, melted
½ cup (125 ml) chopped sweet red pepper

Grease or line muffin cups with paper liners; set aside.

In large bowl, whisk together cornmeal, flour, coriander, baking powder, baking soda and salt. In separate bowl, whisk together eggs, buttermilk and butter; pour over dry ingredients. Sprinkle with red pepper; stir just until moistened. Spoon into prepared cups.

Bake in centre of 400°F (200°C) oven until tops are firm to the touch, about 25 minutes. Let stand in pan for 2 minutes. Serve warm or transfer to rack to let cool.

Note: To Make-ahead: Store in airtight container for up to 24 hours or wrap individually in plastic wrap and freeze in airtight container for up to 2 weeks.

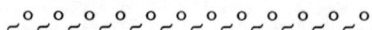

TIP:

A teaspoon of sugar mixed with your yeast and water makes it raise better. Even if you are making bread you can use some sugar. Never mix salt directly with the yeast and water mixture as the salt kills the raising action.

Honey-Buttermilk Cornbread

2 cups stone ground cornmeal
1 cup all-purpose flour
2 ½ teaspoons baking powder
½ teaspoon baking soda
¾ teaspoon salt
2 large eggs
¾ cup buttermilk
¾ cup milk
3 tablespoons honey
¼ cup melted butter, cooled

Heat oven to 400 °F. Grease a 9 inches square baking pan or spray with non-stick baking spray.

In a medium bowl, combine the cornmeal, flour, baking powder, soda, and salt.

In another bowl, whisk together the eggs, buttermilk, milk, honey, and melted butter.

Stir the liquid mixture into the dry mixture until blended. Spread in the prepared baking pan.

Bake for 25-35 minutes, or until the top is golden brown.

Italian Bread

¼ cup sun-dried tomatoes, chopped
2½ cups all purpose flour
2 tablespoons white sugar
2 teaspoons baking powder
½ teaspoon baking soda
¼ teaspoon salt
1 teaspoon dried rosemary
2 tablespoons dried parsley
1 cup sharp Cheddar cheese, grated

¼ cup green onions, chopped
1 egg
1½ cups buttermilk
3 tablespoons olive oil
1 clove garlic, crushed

Preheat oven to 350 °F (175 °C). Grease a 9 x 5 loaf pan.

Whisk together the oil, egg, and buttermilk in a small bowl.

In a large bowl, whisk together flour, sugar, baking powder, soda, salt, and dried herbs. Stir in cheese and onions. Pour buttermilk mixture into the flour mixture, and stir to combine. Add garlic and tomatoes until evenly distributed. Spread batter into prepared pan. Smooth top, and tap pan on counter to remove bubbles.

Bake for 60-65 minutes, until golden. Cool loaf on wire rack.

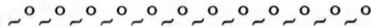

Berry Ricotta Muffins

1 cup (250 ml) whole wheat flour
1 cup (250 ml) unbleached all-purpose flour
½ cup (125 ml) oatmeal
¼ cup (60 ml) wheat or oat bran
2 tablespoons (30 ml) ground flax seeds (optional)
1 tablespoon (15 ml) baking powder
1 teaspoon (5 ml) baking soda
½ teaspoon (2 ml) salt
½ cup (125 ml) soft butter
½ cup (125 ml) brown sugar
2 eggs
1 cup (250 ml) Ricotta cheese
½ cup (125 ml) milk
1 cup (250 ml) frozen berries

Honey & Ricotta spread:
1 cup (250 ml) Ricotta cheese
2 tablespoons (30 ml) honey
Cinnamon to taste (optional)

Preheat oven to 350 °F (180°C).

Grease and flour muffin moulds or line with paper cups.

In a large mixing bowl, mix dry ingredients and create a well in the middle.

In a separate bowl, mix brown sugar and soft butter. Add eggs one by one, mixing thoroughly after each. Add Ricotta and milk, and mix.

Pour liquid mix gradually into dry preparation, mixing with a fork to ensure a homogenous texture. Add fruit and mix again.

Spread dough into muffin moulds and bake in oven centre 15-20 minutes or until golden and a toothpick comes out of muffin clean.

Meanwhile, prepare muffin spread. Serve warm or at room temperature, topped with spread and sprinkled with cinnamon (optional) and accompanied with fresh fruit.

~°~°~°~°~°~°~°~°~°~°~°~°~°~°

"Of all the words of tongue and pen,
The saddest are, "It might have been,"
More sad are these we daily see
"It is, but it hadn't ought to be!"
—John Greenleaf Whittier "Maud Muller"

TIP:

Fill a large hole or sugar shaker with flour and use that when needing to dust surfaces with flour or just pour out a tablespoon as you need it, this is handy way to keep a bit of flour on hand instead of digging in the flour bin.

Sweet and Spicy Guinness Quick Bread

This sweet and spicy quick bread would make a great St. Patrick's Day breakfast, or a heartening snack served with a cup of coffee or Irish tea. The magic ingredient is Guinness stout, a dark Irish beer that adds wonderful moistness and flavour.

2½ cups all-purpose flour
1 teaspoon baking powder
¾ cup organic brown sugar
1 (12-ounces) Guinness or other Irish stout beer, minus a sip (fun for the cook!)
½ cup raisins
2/3 cup walnuts, chopped
1 teaspoon cinnamon

Preheat oven to 350 °F. Combine all ingredients in a mixing bowl, then spoon into a greased loaf pan.

Bake 50 minutes. Serve warm or room temperature.

Makes one loaf.

~°~°~°~°~°~°~°~°~°~°~°~°~°~°

Molasses Doughnuts

¾ cup sugar
3 tablespoons butter, softened
¾ cup milk
2 eggs
¼ cup fancy molasses
3 cups all purpose flour
3 teaspoons baking powder
¼ teaspoon salt
1 teaspoon nutmeg
½ teaspoon cinnamon

Cream sugar and butter together. Add milk, eggs and molasses. Mix well. Mix and sift remaining ingredients. Add to liquid mixture and mix thoroughly. Refrigerate for 1 ½ hours. Turn out on a lightly floured board and roll to ½ inch thick. Cut with doughnut cutter. Fry in deep fryer @375 °F until golden brown, Sprinkle with sugar.

꙳ꞏᵒꞏᵒꞏᵒꞏᵒꞏᵒꞏᵒꞏᵒꞏᵒꞏᵒꞏᵒꞏᵒꞏᵒ

Boston Brown Bread

½ cup (heaping) all-purpose flour
½ cup (heaping) rye flour
½ cup (heaping) finely ground corn meal
½ teaspoon baking powder
½ teaspoon baking soda
½ teaspoon salt
½ teaspoon allspice
½ cup molasses (any kind)
1 cup buttermilk
1 teaspoon vanilla extract (optional)
½ cup raisins (optional)
One metal 6-inch tall by 4-inch diameter coffee can, or a 4x8 loaf pan

You can either make this in the oven or the stovetop, and you can either make this with a loaf pan or a metal coffee can. If you are using the oven method, preheat the oven to 325°F and bring a large pot of water to a boil. If you are using the stovetop method, set the steamer rack inside a tall stockpot and fill the pot with enough water to come 1/3 of the way up the sides of your coffee can. Turn the burner on to medium as you work.

Grease a coffee can or small loaf pan with butter. In a large bowl, mix the all-purpose flour, rye flour, corn meal, baking powder and soda, salt and allspice. Add the raisins if using.

In another bowl, mix together the buttermilk and vanilla extract if using. Whisk in the molasses. Pour the wet ingredients into the dry and stir well with a spoon.

Pour the batter into the coffee can or loaf pan taking care that the batter not reach higher than 2/3 up the sides of the container.

Cover the loaf pan or coffee can tightly with foil. If you are using the stovetop method, set the can in the pot, cover and turn the heat to high. If you are using the oven method, find a high-sided roasting pan that can hold the coffee can or loaf pan. Pour the boiling water into the roasting pan until it reaches one third up the side of the coffee can or loaf pan. Put the roasting pan into the oven. Steam the bread for at least 2 hours and 15 minutes. Check to see if the bread is done by inserting a toothpick into it. If the toothpick comes out clean, you're ready. If not, recover the pan and cook for up to another 45 minutes.

Remove from the oven and let cool for 10 minutes before putting on a rack. Let the bread cool for 1 hour before turning out of the container.

Slice and eat plain, or toast in a little butter in a frying pan.

Serves 4-6.

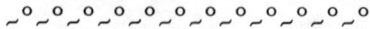

<u>MY SPECIAL RECIPES</u>

Chapter Three

Main Courses

"Tomatoes and oregano make it Italian; wine and tarragon make it French. Sour cream makes it Russian; lemon and cinnamon make it Greek. Soy sauce makes it Chinese; garlic makes it good."—Alice May Brock

Hints:
How to Make Gravy
Making Gravy with Corn Starch:
Remove the roast from the pan. Place pan on stove on medium high heat. Pour off all but 2 tablespoons of the drippings in the pan.

Dissolve 2 tablespoons of corn starch in the minimum amount of water needed to make a thin paste—about ¼ cup. Pour into pan with drippings and use a wire whisk or spatula to blend into the drippings

Stir with a wire whisk until the gravy begins to thicken. As it thickens, slowly add water, stock, milk, or cream, or some combination to the pan. Alternate stirring and adding liquid, maintaining the consistency you want, for several minutes. Add about 2 cups of liquid all together. Yields about 2 cups of gravy. Season with too taste.

Making Gravy with Flour:

Remove the roast from the pan. Place pan on stove on medium high heat. Pour off all but 2 tablespoons of the drippings in the pan.

Into the 2 tablespoons of drippings in the pan stir in 1-2 tablespoons of flour. Stir with a wire whisk until the flour has thickened and the gravy is smooth. Continue to cook slowly to brown the flour, and stir constantly.

Slowly add back some of the previously removed drippings (remove some of the fat beforehand if there is a lot of fat). In addition, add either water, milk, stock, or cream to the gravy, enough to make 2 cups. Season the gravy with salt and pepper and herbs.

~°~°~°~°~°~°~°~°~°~°~°~°~°~°~°

South Carolina Mustard BBQ Sauce:

4 tablespoons butter
½ onion, grated (use a box grater or cheese grater)
½ cup cider vinegar
½ cup brown sugar
½ cup yellow mustard
1 tablespoon dry mustard
1 teaspoon cayenne
1 bay leaf
Salt to taste

Sauté the onions in butter until soft (but not browned), about 3-4 minutes on medium heat. Add the other sauce ingredients and simmer slowly, stirring occasionally, for at least 30 minutes.

~°~°~°~°~°~°~°~°~°~°~°~°~°~°~°

"Life is one fool thing after another where as love is two fool things after each other."
—Oscar Wilde

Black Molasses Ribs

1 tablespoon salad oil
1 medium-sized onion, minced
½ cup molasses
¼ cup honey
½ cup cider vinegar or ½ bottle of beer
1 teaspoon Worcestershire sauce
½ teaspoon salt
¼ teaspoon dry mustard
1 garlic, clove, minced
½ teaspoon horseradish

4 pounds ribs, cut into serving-sized pieces boil until tender in salted water. Drain

Add all other ingredients to a pot and simmer until thickened.

Place ribs on a foil-lined baking sheet in hot oven, slather with ½ of above sauce brown until glazed

Turnover and repeat on other side.

Can be done on BBQ, watch carefully so they don't burn.

~°~°~°~°~°~°~°~°~°~°~°~°~°~°

MY SPECIAL RECIPES

Poultry

Chilled Turkey Loaf

4 pounds turkey drumsticks (about 4 small)
6 cups water
2 chicken bouillon cubes
1 bay leaf
1 teaspoon salt
½ cup dry white wine or 1 tablespoon lemon juice
1 teaspoon Thyme
1 teaspoon sage
2 cloves garlic, minced or pressed
½ cup green onions, chopped
½ cup parsley, chopped
1 (2 ounces) jar pimento, diced
¼ teaspoon black pepper, freshly ground

In a 6 quart kettle, combine the turkey, water, bouillon, bay leaf, and salt. Cover and simmer until meat is very tender and begins to fall away from the bone, about 2½ hours. Lift out meat and set aside to cool. Add wine to cooking liquid and boil, uncovered, until reduced to 3 cups.

Remove meat from the bones, discarding skin, tendons, and bones. Tear meat into fine shreds and combine with the thyme, sage, garlic, onion, parsley, pimento (drained), and black pepper. Pack meat mixture into a 5 x 9 inch loaf pan, pour in the cooking liquid. Cover and chill until set, at least 6 hours.

Run a knife around the pan sides to loosen. Dip pan into hot water for 5 seconds, then invert onto a serving plate and slice.

Serve with bread, lettuce, and condiments for sandwiches, or serve plain. Serves 6.

~°~°~°~°~°~°~°~°~°~°~°~°~°~°~°

Turkey Stew

2 tablespoons olive oil
3 pounds turkey thighs (preferred) or legs (skin on, bone in)
1 medium-large yellow onion, peeled and roughly chopped
2 stalks celery, roughly chopped
1 quart vegetable stock
2 medium carrots, peeled, ¼ inch slices
2-3 medium turnips, peeled, ½ inch cubes
1 medium rutabaga, peeled, ¼ inch slices
3 medium potatoes, peeled and quartered
2 teaspoons salt
1 teaspoon Chicken Spices
Pepper
One Dutch oven with cover.

Preheat oven to 300°F. Heat olive oil on medium high heat in a Dutch oven on the stove top. Wash and pat dry turkey pieces. Brown turkey pieces, skin side down, 2-3 minutes on each side. You may need to brown in batches if necessary. In the last 3 minutes of browning of the last batch, add the onions and celery.

Add salt and ½ of the stock. Bring to a simmer, remove from the stove top and put in the oven, covered, for one hour.

After an hour, remove from oven and add the rest of the vegetables; carrots, turnips, rutabaga, and potatoes, spices, and the rest of the stock. Return to the oven, covered, and cook until tender, another hour or more.

Remove bones and skin, discard. Season to taste.

_°_°_°_°_°_°_°_°_°_°_°_°_°_°_°

Chicken Bacon Roulades

4 shallots, thinly sliced
10 bacon slices (about ½ pound)
4 skinless boneless chicken breast halves (about 1½ pounds)
Lemon pepper seasoning to taste
6 tablespoons (about 1 ounce) Parmesan, grated
1 tablespoon olive oil
1 clove garlic, minced
1/3 cup dry white wine
2 tablespoons butter, unsalted
1½ tablespoons flour
1¼ cups chicken broth
¼ cup heavy cream

Working in batches, cook the bacon over medium heat in an ovenproof heavy skillet, until lightly brown but still flexible (not crisp). Place the bacon on paper towels to drain. Cook the shallots in the remaining bacon fat over low heat, stirring, until softened. Transfer shallots with a slotted spoon to a small bowl and leave any fat remaining in skillet. Preheat oven to 300°F.

Place each chicken breast half between 2 sheets of plastic wrap. With smooth side of a meat pounder pound each breast to 1/8 inch thickness. Discard plastic from boned side of each breast. Sprinkle chicken with lemon pepper and salt. Place 2½ slices of bacon lengthwise along middle of each breast. Top with shallots and Parmesan. Using plastic wrap to help you, tightly roll up each breast lengthwise, tucking in the ends to enclose the filling. Secure seams with wooden toothpicks.

Add 1 tablespoon olive oil to reserved fat in skillet and heat over medium high heat. Brown roulades on all sides, about 5 minutes total. Transfer the skillet to middle of oven and bake roulades until just cooked through, 20-25 minutes.

Transfer chicken to a plate with tongs and keep warm, covered with aluminum foil. Pour off fat from skillet. Add wine to the skillet and deglaze over medium high heat, scraping up brown bits. Boil wine until reduced to about 1 tablespoon. Add garlic and butter. Cook mixture over medium low heat, stirring, for 1 minute. Add flour and cook roux, stirring, 1 minute. Add broth and cream and bring to a boil, whisking. Simmer the sauce, whisking, 2 minutes. Pour through a fine mesh sieve into a small saucepan. Keep sauce warm. Remove the wooden toothpicks from roulades and cut crosswise into ½ inch slices. Spoon some sauce in center of each of 4 plates and arrange roulade slices decoratively on sauce.

~°~°~°~°~°~°~°~°~°~°~°~°~°~°

Stuffed Herbed Chicken

2 skinless, boneless chicken breast halves, 1/2-pound each
Fresh basil leaves, (or other green—beet green, Swiss chard, spinach), enough to cover each chicken breast
2 tablespoons finely chopped toasted walnuts
2.5 ounces herbed cream cheese, room temperature
1/3 cup bread crumbs
3 tablespoons Parmesan cheese, grated
1 egg, beaten well
Salt
Pepper

Herbed Cheese
2.5 oz cream cheese, softened
1 garlic clove, minced
3 teaspoons fresh parsley, minced
3 teaspoons fresh chives, minced pinch of cayenne

¼ teaspoon freshly cracked black peppercorns pinch salt

Preheat oven to 350°F. Put each chicken breast half between two layers of plastic wrap, on a chopping board, and use a meat mallet to pound until ¼ inch thick.

Dip each basil (or other bitter green) leaf in boiling water, drain and set aside.

Mix together the Herbed Cheese ingredients. Mix the walnuts into the cheese mixture, set aside.

Lay the chicken breasts flat, season each side with salt and pepper. Spread the cheese-walnut mixture over each breast, covering the surface of the breasts. Layer on the basil leaves. Starting at the shortest end of the chicken breast, roll up as tightly as possible and tuck in the ends to form a neat roll. Secure each breast with 2 toothpicks.

Put flour, beaten egg, and bread crumbs combined with the Parmesan cheese on to 3 separate flat dishes. Dredge each chicken breast roll first in the flour, then the egg, and finally the Parmesan bread crumbs.

(Skip this step if you are going low carb and/or gluten-free.)

Transfer chicken breasts to a greased baking dish, seam side down. Bake @ 350°F for 40-50 minutes, depending on the size of the breast, until the internal temperature is 165°F, the juices run clear, and the chicken is slightly browned.

Let stand for 5 minutes before serving.

TIP:
Blender and The Mason Jar
Remove the base from the regular blender container.
Screw on the base to the mason jar. Make sure it is nice and tight.
Invert the jar and place on the blender.

Use as you would a food processor. Pulse or blend to desired degree.

Remove mason jar and put a lid on it. Airtight and no extra mess.

Easy Turkey Pot Pie

3 cups cubed cooked turkey
1/2 small onion, chopped
1 (10.75 ounces) can cream of potato soup
1 (10.75 ounces) can cream of chicken soup
1/2 (10.75 ounces) can water
2 (15 ounces) cans mixed vegetables, drained salt and pepper to taste
1 teaspoon Worcestershire sauce
1 frozen 9 inch pie crust

Heat the oven to 400 °F. Let the pie crust stand at room temperature for 15 minutes or until it's easy to handle.

Put the onions, vegetables and poultry in a 9 inch deep dish pie plate or 1½ quart baking dish.

Stir the soup, water, Worcestershire sauce, salt and pepper in a medium bowl. Pour the soup mixture over the poultry mixture. Gently put the pie crust over the poultry mixture. Crimp or roll the edges to seal it to the dish. Cut slits in the crust with a knife.

Bake for 35 minutes or until hot and the crust is golden brown.

<u>MY SPECIAL RECIPES</u>

<u>Beef</u>

"Let go of old expectations, forget the tried and true of the past and have a little fun playing in the kitchen"

Hint:
<u>*Chimichurri Sauce*</u>
1½ cups firmly packed fresh flat-leaf parsley, trimmed of thick stems
4-6 garlic cloves
3 tablespoons fresh oregano leaves
3 tablespoons red or white wine vinegar
¾ cup olive oil
1½ teaspoon sea salt
½ teaspoon red pepper flakes
¼ teaspoon freshly ground black pepper

Prepare the chimichurri sauce/marinade. Finely chop the parsley, garlic and oregano (can do with a food processor), place in a small bowl. Stir in the vinegar, oil, salt, pepper, and red pepper flakes. Set aside two thirds of the sauce for serving with a steak (cover with plastic wrap and let sit at room temperature). The remaining third of the sauce will be for the marinade.

o ͜ o ͜ o ͜ o ͜ o ͜ o ͜ o ͜ o ͜ o ͜ o ͜ o

Beef Goulash with Dumplings

Goulash: 2 tablespoons extra virgin olive oil
4 cups onions, thinly sliced
1 tablespoon sugar
3 garlic cloves, minced
1 tablespoon caraway seeds, toasted and ground
1½ tablespoons sweet Hungarian paprika
1 teaspoon spicy Hungarian paprika
2 tablespoons minced fresh marjoram leaves
1 teaspoon minced fresh thyme leaves
1 bay leaf
3 tablespoon tomato paste
2 tablespoon balsamic vinegar
4 cups chicken stock
2½ pounds chuck roast, cut into 2-inch cubes (remove excess fat)
1 teaspoon kosher salt
¼ teaspoon freshly ground black pepper

Dumplings: 2 cups cake flour
2 teaspoons baking powder
1 teaspoon salt
¾ cup milk
2 tablespoons melted butter

In a large covered sauté pan, heat the olive oil and sauté the onions and sugar until caramelized. Add the garlic and caraway seed. Cook another minute.

Add the sweet and spicy paprika, marjoram, thyme and bay leaf. Sauté another minute, until fragrant.

Add the tomato paste. Deglaze with the vinegar and the stock and add the pieces of beef, salt and pepper. Bring to a boil, then lower to a simmer. Cover and cook until very tender, about 1½ hours, stirring occasionally. Taste and adjust seasoning with salt and pepper.

To prepare the dumplings, sift together the cake flour, baking powder and salt. Combine with the milk and melted butter, mixing lightly. After the stew has cooked until tender, drop the dumpling batter by (heaping) teaspoonfuls into the simmering stew. Cover and cook for 15 minutes. Once you have covered the pan, do *not* uncover while the dumplings are cooking! In order for them to be light and fluffy, they must steam. If you uncover the pan, the steam will escape and the dumplings will boil instead. After 15 minutes, test the dumplings with a toothpick. If the toothpick comes out clean, the dumplings are done.

₋°₋°₋°₋°₋°₋°₋°₋°₋°₋°₋°₋°₋°

Corned Beef Hash

If you have leftover cabbage from corned beef and cabbage, feel free to chop that up as well and add that to the hash.

2-3 tablespoons unsalted butter
1 medium onion, finely chopped (about 1 cup)
2-3 cups finely chopped, cooked corned beef
2-3 cups chopped cooked potatoes
Salt and pepper
Chopped fresh parsley
Heat butter in a large skillet (preferably cast iron) on medium heat. Add the onion and cook a few minutes, until translucent.

Mix in the chopped corned beef and potatoes. Spread out evenly over the pan. Increase the heat to high or medium high and press down on the mixture with a metal spatula.

Do not stir the potatoes and corned beef, but let them brown. If you hear them sizzling, this is good. Use a metal spatula to peak underneath and see if they are browning. If nicely browned, use the spatula to flip sections over in the pan so that they brown on the other side. Press down again with the spatula. If there is too much sticking, you can add a little more butter to the pan. Continue to cook in this manner until the potatoes and the corned beef are nicely browned.

Remove from heat, stir in chopped parsley. Add plenty of freshly ground black pepper, and add salt to taste.

Serve with fried or poached eggs for breakfast.

˷º˷º˷º˷º˷º˷º˷º˷º˷º˷º˷º˷º˷º˷º˷º

TIP:
To cook hamburgers in a hurry, poke a hole in the center when shaping. The centers will cook more quickly and when the hamburgers are done, the holes are gone.

<u>*Blue Cheese Burgers*</u>
1 pound ground beef, lean
1 tablespoon Dijon mustard
2 cloves minced garlic
2 green onions, chopped
½ cup (2 ounces) crumbled blue cheese
1 egg
1 tablespoon water
½ tablespoon Worcestershire sauce
Salt and freshly ground black pepper

Put ground beef, mustard, garlic, onions, blue cheese, water and egg into a large bowl. Use your hands to gently mix the ingredients together until just mixed. Do not over-mix. Shape into patties, about ½ inch thick and larger than your bun. Chill until you are ready to cook.

Prepare BBQ for cooking over high direct heat. Make sure grill is hot and well oiled before laying down the patties. Season patties with salt and pepper. Grill the burgers for about 5 minutes per side. Do not press down on the burgers while cooking.

For indoor cooking a grill pan or a cast iron frying pan can be used.

Serve on hamburger buns with garnish of choice.

Makes 4 burgers.

୦ ୦ ୦ ୦ ୦ ୦ ୦ ୦ ୦ ୦ ୦ ୦ ୦ ୦ ୦

Chili-Crusted Tri-Tip Roast

1 (3-4 pound) beef tri-tip roast
Salt and pepper

Rub:
1 tablespoon chili powder
2 teaspoons ground cumin
1 teaspoon onion powder
1/2 teaspoon garlic powder
1/4 teaspoon pepper

Heat oven to 425 °F. Combine rub ingredients in small bowl; press evenly onto all surfaces of beef roast.

Place roast on rack in shallow roasting pan. Do not add water or cover. Roast in 425 °F oven 30-40 minutes for medium rare; 40-45 minutes for medium doneness.

Remove roast when instant-read thermometer registers 135 °F for medium rare; 150 °F for medium. Transfer roast to carving board; tent loosely with aluminum foil. Let stand 15 minutes. (Temperature will continue to rise about 10 °F to reach 145 °F for medium rare; 160 °F for medium.)

Carve roast across the grain into thin slices. Season with salt and pepper, as desired.

୦ ୦ ୦ ୦ ୦ ୦ ୦ ୦ ୦ ୦ ୦ ୦ ୦ ୦

Chinese Pot Roast

1 (4 pound) boneless beef chuck roast
1 tablespoon garlic salt
1 tablespoon ground black pepper
1 teaspoon dry mustard powder
1 tablespoon vegetable oil
3 cups water
3/4 cup soy sauce
3 tablespoons white vinegar
1/4 cup honey
1 teaspoon ground ginger
1 teaspoon celery seed
2 tablespoons cornstarch
1/4 cup cold water

Preheat the oven to 325 °F (165 °C).

Coat the chuck roast with garlic salt, pepper and mustard powder. Heat the oil in a large oven-proof skillet or Dutch oven over medium-high heat. Add the roast and brown on both sides, about 5 minutes per side.

In a medium bowl, stir together 3 cups of water, soy sauce, vinegar, honey, ginger and celery seed. Pour over the roast and then cover the roast tightly with a lid or aluminum foil.

Bake in the preheated oven until the roast is very tender, 2 ½-3 hours.

When the roast is done, remove it from the pan to a serving plate. Set the pan of drippings over medium-high heat and bring to a boil. Stir together cornstarch and ¼ cup of cold water. Pour into the boiling liquid and stir until thickened, about 1 minute. Serve the roast with the gravy poured over.

~°~°~°~°~°~°~°~°~°~°~°~°~°

Easy Beef Pot Pie

1 refrigerated pie crust
2 cups diced cooked potatoes
1 (10 ounces) package frozen mixed vegetables, thawed
1½ cups diced cooked beef
1 (10.75 ounces) can Campbell's® Condensed Golden Mushroom Soup
1/3 cup water
1 teaspoon Worcestershire sauce
1 teaspoon dried thyme leaves, crushed

Heat the oven to 400 °F. Let the pie crust stand at room temperature for 15 minutes or until it's easy to handle.

Put the potatoes, vegetables and beef in a 9 inches deep-dish pie plate or 1 ½ quart baking dish.

Stir the soup, water, Worcestershire and thyme in a medium bowl. Pour the soup mixture over the beef mixture. Gently put the pie crust over the beef mixture. Crimp or roll the edges to seal it to the dish. Cut slits in the crust with a knife.

Bake for 35 minutes or until hot and the crust is golden brown.

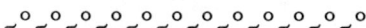

Beef Puff

1 cup cooked beef, finely chopped
2 tablespoons onions, chopped
2 medium potatoes
1 teaspoon salt
¼ cup milk
1 egg, slightly beaten
¼ cup cheese, grated
1-1½ teaspoon margarine

Wash and peel potatoes. Cook until tender. Drain and mash. Beat together mashed potatoes, onion, salt, milk and egg.

Fold beef into potato mixture. Turn into greased casserole. Top with grated cheese and dot with margarine.

Bake @ 400 °F for ½ hour and serve hot.

~°~°~°~°~°~°~°~°~°~°~°~°~°~°

Home Cured Corned Beef

The spice mix with the gallon of brine makes easily enough curing brine for a 5 pound brisket, cured in a somewhat larger container. If you were to use a 2-gallon freezer bag or marinating bag, you would likely need just half (or less) of the amount of brine and brine spices.

Pickling spices:
1 tablespoon whole allspice berries
1 tablespoon whole mustard seeds (brown or yellow)
1 tablespoon coriander seeds
1 tablespoon red pepper flakes
1 tablespoon whole cloves
1 tablespoon whole black peppercorns
9 whole cardamom pods
6 large bay leaves, crumbled
2 teaspoons ground ginger
½ stick cinnamon

Brine:
1 gallon water
2 cups Kosher salt
5 teaspoons pink curing salt
3 tablespoons pickling spices
½ cup brown sugar

Note: Pink curing salt. If you don't have it, you can still make corned beef, but it is necessary for that vibrant pink color we associate with corned beef. And it adds flavour too. Without it the corned beef will be a dull grey color.

Brisket:
4-5 pound beef brisket
1 tablespoon pickling spices

You can either used store-bought pickling spices or you can make your own. To make your own, toast the allspice berries, mustard seeds, coriander seeds, red pepper flakes, cloves, peppercorns, and cardamom pods in a small frying pan on high heat until fragrant and you hear the mustard seeds start to pop. Remove from heat and place in a small bowl. Use a mortar and pestle to crush the spices a little (or the back of a spoon or the side of a knife on a flat surface). Add to a small bowl and stir in the crumbled bay leaves and ground ginger.

Add about 3 tablespoons of the spice mix (reserve the rest for cooking the corned beef after it has cured), plus the half stick of cinnamon, to a gallon of water in a large pot, along with the Kosher salt, pink salt, and brown sugar. Bring to a boil, then remove from heat and let cool to room temperature. Then refrigerate until well chilled.

Place the brisket in a large, flat container or pan, and cover with the brine. The brine should cover the meat. The meat may float in which case you may want to weigh it down with a plate. Alternatively you can use a 2-gallon freezer bag (placed in a container so if it leaks it doesn't leak all over your refrigerator), place the brisket in the freezer bag and about 2 quarts of brine, squeezing out the air from the bag before sealing. Place in the refrigerator and chill from 5-7 days. Every day flip the brisket over, so that all sides get brined equally.

At the end of the cure, remove the brisket from the brine and rinse off the brine with cold water. Place the brisket in a large pot that just fits around the brisket and cover with at least one inch of water. If you want your brisket less salty, add another inch of water to the pot. Add a tablespoon of the pickling spices to the pot. Bring to a boil, reduce to a very low simmer (barely bubbling), and cook 3-4 hours, until the corned beef is fork tender. (At this point you can store in the fridge for up to a week.) Remove the meat to a cutting board. (You can use the spiced cooking liquid to cook vegetables for boiled dinner or corned beef and cabbage.) Slice thinly against the grain to serve.

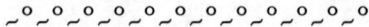

<u>MY SPECIAL RECIPES</u>

Pork

Cranberry Apple Stuffed Pork Loin

1 boneless pork loin (about 3 pounds)
Sea salt and freshly ground pepper
1 cup seasoned croutons
½ cup chicken stock
1 cup peeled, chopped green apples
1/3 cup dried cranberries
1/3 cup chopped walnuts, toasted
¼ cup minced shallots
2 tablespoons pure maple syrup
1 teaspoon minced rosemary

Preheat oven to 325°F.

Rinse the pork and pat it dry. Butterfly the roast by first cutting lengthwise about halfway through the roast. Then angle the knife and cut horizontally almost all of the way through, on both sides. Unfold the pork and cut tiny slits in the surface of the meat. Cover with 2 layers of plastic wrap. Pound with a meat mallet to flatten as much as possible. Remove plastic wrap. Sprinkle pork with salt and pepper and set aside.

Place croutons and stock in a small bowl and let sit for 5 minutes, until the croutons have absorbed the stock and have softened. Mash up the croutons a bit with a fork. Stir in the apples, walnuts, cranberries, shallots, maple syrup and rosemary. Spread mixture over surface of the pork. Starting with the smallest side of the meat (which should be in the shape of a rectangle), roll up tightly and secure with kitchen string.

Note: *At this point you can wrap in plastic wrap and refrigerate if you are making ahead.*

Coat the bottom of a roasting pan with cooking spray or a little olive oil. Place the roast in the pan and cook @ 325 °F, uncovered, for about 1 hour ten minutes, or until the pork reaches an internal temperature of 140-145 °F. Start checking the internal temperature of the roast at about one hour. Let stand for 10 minutes. Remove the kitchen string and slice into ½ inch thick slices.

~°~°~°~°~°~°~°~°~°~°~°~°~°~°~°

Pork Chow Mein

1 pound lean pork tenderloin cut into thin strips
1 tablespoon vegetable oil
2 tablespoons soy sauce + 2 cups beef broth
2 medium celery stalks, chopped
1/2 cup onions, chopped
1 (4 ounces) can mushrooms, reserve juice
3 tablespoons cornstarch
1 (16 ounces) can Chinese vegetables, drained
1 tablespoon brown gravy
3 cups chow mien noodles

In a large skillet or Wok, brown lean pork strips in vegetable oil over medium heat. Once brown, add beef broth, soy sauce, celery and onion. bring heat to boiling. Reduce to simmer, cover and cook 30 minutes. Mix reserved mushroom juice and cornstarch vigorously in sealed container. Blend into pork mixture. Now add mushrooms, Chinese vegetables and brown gravy. Bring heat to boil stirring constantly for 1-2 minutes. Serve over noodles or toss with noodles for 1 minute.

~°~°~°~°~°~°~°~°~°~°~°~°~°~°~°

Orange Pork

1½ pound lean pork strips
1 teaspoon extra virgin olive oil
½ cup fresh orange juice
½ cup fresh pineapple juice
2 garlic cloves, minced
2 teaspoons cornstarch
1 teaspoon orange peel, grated
1½ teaspoons dried basil leaves
Salt and pepper to taste
2 medium oranges, sliced
¾ cup green onions, sliced

In a large cooking pan, heat the olive oil on medium to high heat. Add the pork and cook for 4 to 5 minutes until cooked. In a mixing bowl add in the pineapple and orange juice, minced garlic, cornstarch, and basil, stirring until it is all very well blended. Add the content of the bowl to the pork, bring to a boil then let it cool for 3-4 minutes while stirring. Now salt and pepper the meat, and place it on a bed of rice. Pour the orange basil sauce over pork and rice and let cool.

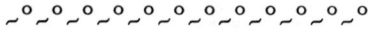

Sweet And Sour Pork

2 pounds sliced lean pork tenderloin
2 tablespoons extra virgin olive oil
1 can pineapple, sliced
¾ cup mineral water
¼ cup apple vinegar
1 tablespoon teriyaki sauce
¼ cup brown sugar, packed
½ teaspoon salt
2 tablespoons corn syrup

1 large onion, diced
2 green peppers, sliced
2 cups white rice, cooked

Sliced up the seasoned lean pork tenderloin into strips, and sauté in the extra virgin olive oil on high until thoroughly cooked. Once the meat is well cooked, add in the rest of the fresh ingredients, and cook until the veggies are slightly browned. Cook 2 cups of white rice.

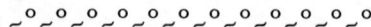

German Pork Hocks

3 lean pork hocks
1 large onion, chopped
3 large carrots, sliced
2 celery stalks, sliced
5 garlic cloves, minced
2 fresh leeks, sliced
1 teaspoon salt
1 teaspoon black pepper
1 teaspoon fresh peppercorns
2 tablespoons vegetable shortening
1 cup beer

Begin this recipe by slicing up the leeks, onions, and fresh carrots. In a large soup pot, cook all of the listed ingredients for 3 hours. Once done, drain the water. Now, you will want to preheat your oven to 400 °F.

Liquefy the vegetable shortening in cooking iron skillet. Now bake everything together for about 25 minutes. Make sure you check it frequently, as you want the meat and veggies to remain moist with flavour. Serve hot with boiled fresh potatoes.

ᵒ ᵒ ᵒ ᵒ ᵒ ᵒ ᵒ ᵒ ᵒ ᵒ ᵒ ᵒ ᵒ ᵒ

<u>TIP</u>:
Add two teaspoons of vinegar to jello and it will keep the jello from melting when you serve it.

ᵒ ᵒ ᵒ ᵒ ᵒ ᵒ ᵒ ᵒ ᵒ ᵒ ᵒ ᵒ ᵒ ᵒ

<u>Pork Chops with Dijon Sauce</u>

1 tablespoon butter
1 tablespoon olive oil
4 center-cut rib or loin pork chops, boneless or bone-in, about 1 ¼ inches thick
Salt
Freshly ground black pepper
¼ cup chopped shallots or green onions
1 cup dry white wine
¾ cup chicken stock*
¾ cup heavy cream
2 tablespoon Dijon mustard
1 tablespoon chopped parsley (optional)

*If cooking gluten-free, use homemade chicken stock or gluten-free packaged stock.

Pat the pork chops dry with paper towels. Sprinkle salt and pepper all over them. Heat the olive oil in a large skillet over medium high heat. Stir in the butter. As soon as the butter has melted, add the pork chops to the pan and sear them, about 2-3 minutes on each side. Reduce the heat slightly if the chops brown too quickly.

Remove the pork chops from the pan and pour off most of the fat. Add the green onions or shallots and cook them on med high heat until softened, about 1 minute. Add ½ cup of the wine and bring to a boil, deglazing the pan by scraping the brown bits from the bottom of the pan. Stir in the stock and return chops to the pan. Bring sauce to a simmer, reduce heat, cover and cook until chops are cooked through (145°F internal temp), about 10-15 minutes.

Remove the pork chops to a warm platter; cover with foil to keep warm. Add the remaining half cup of wine. Increase the heat to high to boil the pan juices. Reduce the juices by half, about 3 minutes. Add the heavy cream and boil 3 minutes more, until sauce reduces and thickens, and scraping the pan with a wooden spoon leaves a trail. Remove from the heat and whisk in the mustard and parsley. If you want, add more mustard to taste. Place chops on a bed of sauce and serve.

꙰꙰꙰꙰꙰꙰꙰꙰꙰꙰꙰꙰꙰꙰

Studenetz (Jellied Meat)

3 pigs' feet
3 pork hocks
1 tablespoon salt
4 celery stalks and leaves
1 medium onion
1 clove garlic
Pickling spice

Scrape and wash the pigs' feet very thoroughly. Cut the feet in half lengthwise.

Wash the hocks. Place the meat in a large pot and add salt. Cover with cold water and bring to a boil. Skim, cover and simmer very slowly. This is very important. Rapid boiling will make the broth milky.

After 4 hours of simmering, add the whole vegetables and spices. Continue cooking slowly until the meat comes off the bones easily. Separate the meat from the bones (cut it as fine as you wish). Strain the juice and pour over the meat. Chill thoroughly. Meat and juice has to set like jelly.

Note: Remove the fat from the top, before serving. Serve in slices or squares.

~°~°~°~°~°~°~°~°~°~°~°~°~°~°

Spareribs and Sauerkraut

6-7 lbs. "Country Style" pork ribs or boneless pork
½ teaspoon black pepper, coarse ground
1 teaspoon salt
1 large can sauerkraut or deli plastic bag style
1 ½ cup apples, chopped (yellow delicious or Granny Smith are best)
¾ cup onion, chopped
2 teaspoons cloves, ground
1 tablespoon cinnamon
1 teaspoon nutmeg
1 teaspoon dry mustard
1 garlic clove, diced
½ cup brown sugar
¼ cup dark molasses
¼ teaspoon black pepper
1 ½ cups chicken broth

Preheat broiler, dust with ½ teaspoon pepper, 1 teaspoon dry mustard and 1 teaspoon salt and brown all sides of ribs (in a deep Dutch oven or slow cooker), reduce oven to 350 °F

Drain sauerkraut. Place on top of browned ribs. Mix spices, apples, onion, garlic, sugar and molasses and place on top of sauerkraut and ribs. Pour chicken broth on top. Cover and bake 2 hours in oven or longer in slow cooker. Serve topped with sour cream.

~°~°~°~°~°~°~°~°~°~°~°~°~°~°

<u>MY SPECIAL RECIPES</u>

Seafood and Fish

Hint:
Prepare Fish For Cooking
Put fish on ice immediately after catching them.
Filet or clean fish as soon as possible.
Put fish in zip-loc bags with a table spoon of salt as soon as cleaned.
Fill bag with water and squeeze all air out before sealing.
Keep bag in refrigerator until 1 hour before cooking.
Drain salt water and soak fish in fresh water for one hour.
Cook with favorite recipe!

Tips:
Filets are not as strong tasting as whole fish.
Be sure to mix salt in water completely before sealing.
Soaking fish in fresh water just before cooking removes most of the salt.

~°~°~°~°~°~°~°~°~°~°~°~°~°~°

Glazed Salmon

½ cup apple cider (not hard cider)
1¼ tablespoons honey
4 skinless salmon fillets (6 ounces each)
1 teaspoon olive oil
Salt and pepper, to taste
2 lemons, cut in half
1 tablespoon butter

12 ounces fresh baby spinach
1½ tablespoons white wine

Preheat oven to 350 °F. Place salmon fillets in a baking dish large enough to hold the salmon in one layer.

In a saucepan over medium-high heat, bring the cider and honey to a boil and let the mixture bubble steadily until it reduces by half.

Pour the cider over the salmon, let it sit for 10 minutes.

Heat olive oil in a large baking dish on medium-high. Sprinkle the flesh side of the salmon fillets with salt and pepper. Place the fish in the pan. Cook for 2 minutes, brushing the top with cider glaze so that the fish begins to caramelize.

Turn the salmon fillets over and brush with the remaining cider glaze. Add the lemon halves to the skillet. Transfer the baking dish to the oven. Bake for 6-8 minutes or until the salmon flakes easily when tested with the tip of a knife.

While the salmon is cooking, in a large skillet over medium-high heat, melt the butter. Add the spinach, salt, and pepper. Cook for 1 minute, or just until the leaves begin to wilt. Pour the wine over them and continue cooking for 1-2 minutes more or until tender.

To serve, drain any excess liquid from the spinach and divide it among 4 plates. Arrange a piece of salmon on top and garnish with a lemon half.

Serves four.

○ ○ ○ ○ ○ ○ ○ ○ ○ ○ ○ ○ ○ ○ ○ ○

Salmon Patties

1 cup mashed potatoes (with milk and butter)
1 (6 ounces) can salmon, drained skin and bones removed
¼ cup onions, chopped
3 saltine crackers, crushed
1 tablespoon fresh parsley, minced

Salt and pepper to taste
1 egg, separated
2 tablespoons cooking oil lemon wedges optional

In a medium bowl, combine potatoes, salmon, onions, cracker crumbs, parsley, salt, pepper and egg yolk; mix well. Beat egg whites until stiff; fold into salmon mixture. Shape into six patties dust each side with very light flour. Heat oil in skillet; fry patties over medium heat 3-4 minutes per side or until golden brown. Garnish with lemon if desired.

Tuna with Peppercorns on a Bed of Greens

2 tuna steaks (1½ pounds)
Salt
2 teaspoons black pepper, coarsely ground
1 tablespoon butter or margarine
1 large onion, thinly sliced
¼ cup dry wine
½ pound fresh kale or spinach, washed
1 tablespoon olive oil
½ teaspoon sugar
¼ teaspoon ground pepper
12 julienne strip carrots
Lemon wedges and purple kale to garnish

Preheat oven to 325°F. Rinse tuna and pat dry with paper towels. Lightly sprinkle fish with salt. Press 2 teaspoons coarsely ground pepper into both sides of steaks; set aside.

Melt butter in large skillet over medium heat. Add onion; cook and stir 5 minutes or until crisp-tender. Add wine and remove from heat. Spread onion mixture on bottom of 9 x 13 inches glass baking dish. Top with fish. Bake 15 minutes. Spoon liquid over fish and bake 15 minutes more or until fish flakes easily when tested with fork.

Meanwhile, trim away tough stems from kale; cut leaves into 1 inch strips. Heat oil in medium skillet over medium-high heat. Add kale, sugar and ¼ teaspoon finely ground black pepper. Cook and stir 2-3 minutes or until tender. Place kale on plates. Top with fish, onion mixture and cat strips. Garnish, if desired. Serve immediately.

~°~°~°~°~°~°~°~°~°~°~°~°~°

Parmesan Baked Fish

1/4 cup milk
2 teaspoons salt
2 pounds thawed fresh or frozen fish fillets
½ cup fine dry bread crumbs
½ teaspoon paprika
¼ cup Parmesan cheese, grated melted butter

Preheat oven to 375 °F. Grease 11 x 8 x 2 inches baking dish.

Blend together the milk and salt in a shallow bowl. Combine bread crumbs, paprika, and Parmesan cheese in another bowl.

Dip fish fillets into milk mixture then into crumb mixture. Arrange in the prepared baking dish. Drizzle melted butter over fillets. Bake for 25-30 minutes, depending on thickness of fillets. Fish should flake easily with a fork when done.

*"Life is too important to be taken
seriously."—Oscar Wilde*

~°~°~°~°~°~°~°~°~°~°~°~°~°

Bouillabaisse

3 pounds of at least 3 different kinds of fish fillets, fresh or quick frozen (thaw first)
½ cup Olive oil
1-2 pounds of oysters, clams, or mussels
1 cup cooked shrimp, crab, or lobster meat, or rock lobster tails
1 cup onions, thinly sliced
4 shallots, thinly sliced or the white parts of 2-3 leeks, thinly sliced
2 cloves garlic, crushed
1 large tomato, chopped, or 1/2 cup canned tomatoes
1 sweet red pepper, chopped
4 stalks celery, thinly sliced
2 inch slice of fennel or 1 teaspoon of fennel seed
3 sprigs fresh thyme or ¾ teaspoon dried thyme
1 bay leaf
2-3 whole cloves
Zest of half an orange
½ teaspoon powdered saffron
2 teaspoons salt
¼ teaspoon black pepper, freshly ground
1 cup chicken or fish broth
2 tablespoons lemon juice
2/3 cup white wine
Sliced French bread

Heat ¼ cup of the olive oil in a large (6 quart) saucepan. When it is hot, add onions and shallots. Sauté for a minute, then add crushed garlic (more or less to taste), and sweet red pepper. Add tomato, celery, and fennel. Stir the vegetables into the oil with a wooden spoon until well coated. Then add another ¼ cup of olive oil, thyme, bay leaf, cloves and the orange zest. Cook until the onion is soft and golden but not brown.

Cut fish fillets into 2 inch pieces. Add the pieces of fish and 2 cups of water to the vegetable mixture. Bring to a boil, then reduce heat and simmer, uncovered, for about 10 minutes. Add oysters, clams or mussels (though these may be omitted if desired) and shrimp, crabmeat or lobster tails, cut into pieces or left whole.

Add saffron, salt, pepper. Add broth, lemon juice, and white wine. Bring to a simmer again and cook about 5 minutes longer.

At serving time taste and correct the seasoning of the broth, adding a little more salt or pepper if need be, and maybe a touch of lemon juice. Into each soup bowl place a thick slice of crusty French bread, plain or slighlty toasted. Spoon the bouillabaisse over the bread. If desired, serve with Sauce Rouille. Serves 6.

Directions for Sauce Rouille:
1 tablespoon hot chicken or fish stock.
2 cloves peeled garlic
1 small red hot pepper
½ teaspoon salt
¼ cup soft white bread, pulled into bits
1/2 cup olive oil

Put hot fish stock into the bottom of a blender. Add garlic and red hot pepper, salt and bread. Blend until very smooth. With the blender still running, add olive oil slowly and stop the blending as soon as the oil disappears.

At serving time pass Rouille in a little bowl along with the bouillabaisse. Each serving is about ½ a teaspoon that you stir into your soup. Use gingerly like Tabasco.

<u>MY SPECIAL RECIPES</u>

Pasta, Casseroles and Crock Pot

"The most remarkable thing about my mother is that for thirty years she served the family nothing but leftovers. The original meal has never been found."—Calvin Trillin

<u>Hint:</u>
Convert Your Favourites

You can adapt many conventional recipes for the slow cooker. Any oven or stovetop recipe that has some moisture in it—whether from water, broth, wine, sauce, or canned soup—should work beautifully in your favorite appliance, just keep these things in mind:

Cut all liquid amounts in half when adjusting for the slow cooker.

The low heat setting is approximately 200 °F (95 °C) and high heat is about 300 °F (150 °C).

For every hour you'd cook something in the oven or on the stove, allow 8 hours on low or 4 hours on high. (When in doubt, turn it on low and leave it all day or overnight.)

$\sim^{\circ}\sim^{\circ}\sim^{\circ}\sim^{\circ}\sim^{\circ}\sim^{\circ}\sim^{\circ}\sim^{\circ}\sim^{\circ}\sim^{\circ}\sim^{\circ}$

Creamy Pasta with Two Cheeses—GF

Coarse salt
12 ounces gluten free pasta
2 tablespoons butter
1 cup half and half
½ cup Romano cheese
½ cup Parmesan cheese
¼ cup fresh parsley, chopped

In a large pot, melt butter over medium heat. Add half and half cream and cheeses; stir to combine, bring to a simmer. Cook pasta as per package. Add pasta and toss to combine. Serve with sprinkles chopped parsley.

~°~°~°~°~°~°~°~°~°~°~°~°~°

Island Kielbasa in a Slow Cooker

2 pounds kielbasa sausage, sliced into ½ inch pieces
2 cups ketchup
2 cups brown sugar
1 (15 ounces) can pineapple chunks, undrained
½ teaspoon Worcestershire sauce

Place the sausage, ketchup, sugar and pineapple in the slow cooker and mix together.
Cook on low setting for 5-6 hours, until sausage is cooked through.

~°~°~°~°~°~°~°~°~°~°~°~°~°

Slow Cooker Pepper Steak
2 pounds beef sirloin, cut into 2 inch strips garlic powder to taste
3 tablespoons vegetable oil
1 cube beef bouillon
¼ cup hot water
1 tablespoon cornstarch
½ cup onion, chopped
2 large green bell peppers, roughly chopped
1 (14.5 ounces) can stewed tomatoes, with liquid
3 tablespoons soy sauce
1 teaspoon white sugar
1 teaspoon salt

Sprinkle strips of sirloin with garlic powder to taste. In a large skillet over medium heat, heat the vegetable oil and brown the seasoned beef strips. Transfer to a slow cooker.

Mix bouillon cube with hot water until dissolved, then mix in cornstarch until dissolved. Pour into the slow cooker with meat. Stir in onion, green peppers, stewed tomatoes, soy sauce, sugar, and salt.

Cover, and cook on High for 3-4 hours, or on Low for 6-8 hours.

~°~°~°~°~°~°~°~°~°~°~°~°~°~°

"If I had my life to live over again, I'd dare to make more mistakes next time."
—Nadine Stair

Slow Cooker Stuffing

1 cup butter or margarine
2 cups onions, chopped
2 cups celery, chopped
¼ cup fresh parsley, chopped
12 ounces sliced mushrooms
12 cups dry bread cubes
1 teaspoon poultry seasoning
1½ teaspoons dried sage
1 teaspoon dried thyme
½ teaspoon dried marjoram
1½ teaspoons salt
½ teaspoon ground black pepper
4½ cups chicken broth, or as needed
2 eggs, beaten

Melt butter or margarine in a skillet over medium heat. Cook onion, celery, mushroom, and parsley in butter, stirring frequently.

Spoon cooked vegetables over bread cubes in a very large mixing bowl. Season with poultry seasoning, sage, thyme, marjoram, and salt and pepper. Pour in enough broth to moisten, and mix in eggs. Transfer mixture to slow cooker, and cover.

Cook on High for 45 minutes, then reduce heat to Low, and cook for 4-8 hours.

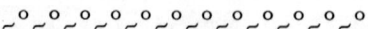

Slow Cooker Barbecue Beef

3 tablespoons all-purpose flour
3 pounds chuck roast
15 ounces tomato sauce
½ cup chopped onion

1/3 cup brown sugar
2 cubes beef bouillon
1½ teaspoons chili powder
1 clove garlic, minced
1 teaspoon mustard powder

Rub the flour into the roast. Place roast in bottom of slow cooker. Pour in the tomato sauce, onion, brown sugar, bouillon, chili powder, garlic and mustard powder. Mix well.

Cover slow cooker and cook on high setting for 8 hours or on low setting for 14-16 hours.

~°~°~°~°~°~°~°~°~°~°~°~°~°~°

Sausage and Bow-tie Pasta Florentine

1 pound hot Italian sausage links
1 (12 ounces) package bow-tie pasta (farfalle)
1 (10 ounces) package frozen chopped spinach, thawed and drained
1 tablespoon olive oil
3 cloves garlic, chopped
1 (16 ounces) jar Alfredo sauce
½ teaspoon black pepper

Preheat the oven's broiler and set the oven rack at about 6 inches from the heat source. Place the sausage links onto a broiler pan, and broil in the preheated oven until the sausage is crispy on the outside and no longer pink on the inside, about 8 minutes. Turn the sausage once as it cooks.

Bring a large pot of lightly salted water to a boil. Add the bow-tie pasta, and cook until al dente, 8-10 minutes. Drain and return to the pot along with the spinach; keep warm over medium-low heat.

Heat the olive oil in a separate pot over medium heat, and stir in the garlic, and cook until the garlic softens and the aroma mellows, about 3 minutes. Add the Alfredo sauce and black pepper, then bring to a simmer over medium-high heat. Cut the cooked sausage into bite-sized pieces, and add to the simmering Alfredo sauce along with the pasta and spinach. Stir until the pasta is hot and well coated with the sauce.

 ͜ ο ͜ ο ͜ ο ͜ ο ͜ ο ͜ ο ͜ ο ͜ ο ͜ ο ͜ ο ͜ ο ͜ ο

Cabbage and Smoked Sausage Pasta

1 (16 ounces) package farfalle (bow tie) pasta
½ cup butter
2 cloves garlic, minced
¼ cup olive oil
1 large head green cabbage, shredded salt and pepper to taste
1 pound smoked sausage, sliced
¼ cup grated Parmesan cheese

Fill a large pot with lightly salted water and bring to a rolling boil over high heat. Once the water is boiling, stir in the bow tie pasta and return to a boil. Cook the pasta uncovered, stirring occasionally, until the pasta has cooked through, but is still firm to the bite, about 12 minutes. Drain well in a colander set in the sink.

Melt the butter in a large pot over medium heat. Add the garlic, olive oil, and cabbage; season with salt and pepper; cook until tender, about 15 minutes. Stir in the sausage and bow tie pasta; cook until completely heated, about 5 minutes more. Top with Parmesan cheese and serve immediately.

 ͜ ο ͜ ο ͜ ο ͜ ο ͜ ο ͜ ο ͜ ο ͜ ο ͜ ο ͜ ο ͜ ο ͜ ο

Smoked Sausage with Pasta

4 ounces angel hair pasta, uncooked
½ pound reduced-fat smoked turkey sausage, cut into ½ inch slices
2 cups fresh mushrooms, sliced
2 garlic cloves, minced
4½ teaspoons fresh basil, minced
1 tablespoon olive or canola oil
1 cup plum tomatoes, julienned, seeded
1/8 teaspoon salt
1/8 teaspoon pepper

Cook pasta as per package directions. Meanwhile, in a large non-stick skillet, sauté the sausage, mushrooms, garlic and basil in oil until mushrooms are tender. Drain pasta; add to the sausage mixture. Add the tomatoes, salt and pepper; toss gently. Heat through.

Greek Pasta with Tomatoes and White Beans

2 (14.5 ounces) cans Italian-style diced tomatoes
1 (19 ounces) can cannellini beans, drained and rinsed
10 ounces fresh spinach, washed and chopped
8 ounces penne pasta
½ cup crumbled feta cheese

Cook the pasta in a large pot of boiling salted water until al dente.

Meanwhile, combine tomatoes and beans in a large non-stick skillet. Bring to a boil over medium high heat. Reduce heat, and simmer 10 minutes.

Add spinach to the sauce; cook for 2 minutes or until spinach wilts, stirring constantly.

Serve sauce over pasta, and sprinkle with feta.

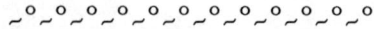

Spaghetti Carbonara

1 pound spaghetti
1 tablespoon olive oil
8 slices bacon, diced
1 tablespoon olive oil
1 onion, chopped
1 clove garlic, minced
¼ cup dry white wine (optional)
4 eggs
½ cup grated Parmesan cheese salt and black pepper to taste
2 tablespoons fresh parsley, chopped
2 tablespoons Parmesan cheese, grated

In a large pot of boiling salted water, cook spaghetti pasta until al dente. Drain well. Toss with 1 tablespoon of olive oil, and set aside.

In a large skillet, cook chopped bacon until slightly crisp; remove and drain onto paper towels. Reserve 2 tablespoons of bacon fat; add remaining 1 tablespoon olive oil, and heat in reused large skillet. Add chopped onion, and cook over medium heat until onion is translucent. Add minced garlic, and cook 1 minute more. Add wine if desired; cook one more minute.

Return cooked bacon to pan; add cooked and drained spaghetti. Toss to coat and heat through, adding more olive oil if it seems dry or is sticking together. Add beaten eggs and cook, tossing constantly with tongs or large fork until eggs are barely set. Quickly add ½ cup Parmesan cheese, and toss again. Add salt and pepper to taste (remember that bacon and Parmesan are very salty).

Serve immediately with chopped parsley sprinkled on top, and extra Parmesan cheese at table.

MY SPECIAL RECIPES

Foreign Dishes

Chicken Cacciatore (Hunter Style Chicken)

One 3 1/2 pound chicken, cut into pieces
2 tablespoons extra virgin olive oil
1 cup onions, thinly sliced
2 garlic cloves, thinly sliced
Salt and freshly ground pepper
1/3 cup white wine
2 cups peeled and chopped, firm ripe tomatoes (or canned plum tomatoes in their juice)

Rinse chicken and pat dry. Heat olive oil in a large skillet on medium heat, add the onions and cook until translucent, stirring occasionally. Push the onions to the side. Add the garlic and chicken pieces, skin-side down. Cook until the chicken skin is golden brown, turn pieces over and brown on the other side.

Season chicken with salt and pepper, on both sides. Add wine and simmer until reduced by half. Add the tomatoes, lower the heat and cover the skillet with the lid slightly ajar.

Cook the chicken in the simmering liquid, turning and basting from time to time. Cook until the thighs are very tender and the meat is almost falling off the bones, about 40 minutes. If the stew ever starts to dry out, add a couple tablespoons of water.

Cardamom Honey Chicken

Marinade: 4 tablespoons honey
2 tablespoons sherry
1 teaspoon cardamom seeds, ground
1 teaspoon peppercorns, ground
Chicken: 6 chicken breasts, or one whole chicken, cut into parts
2 tablespoons Olive oil
1 lemon, thinly sliced
Salt and pepper

Preheat oven to 390 °F. Warm the honey, stir in the sherry, cardamom and peppercorns. Place marinade and chicken in a large bowl, coat chicken with marinade. Cover with plastic wrap and let sit at room temperature for 30 minutes.

Heat olive oil in a large frying pan at medium high heat. Sear the chicken, skin side down, until golden.

Place lemon slices in a roasting pan. Lay the chicken pieces on top. Brush with the marinade. Season generously with salt and pepper. Place in the oven and bake until done, approximately 15 minutes for breasts, 20 minutes for thighs, wings, and drumsticks. Remove from oven and let rest for 10 minutes before serving. Pour out drippings from the pan into a gravy boat for gravy.

Serve with rice, mashed potatoes, or couscous.

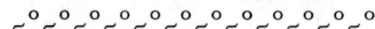

Jamaican Jerk Burgers

2 teaspoons white vinegar
1 tablespoon water
½ chili pepper, seeds removed, minced
½ cup chopped green onion, including greens
2 cloves garlic, chopped
1 tablespoon fresh thyme

1 teaspoon ground allspice
1 teaspoon ground cinnamon
½ teaspoon ground nutmeg
1 teaspoon ground ginger
1 teaspoon molasses
½ teaspoon salt
½ teaspoon freshly ground black pepper
1 ½ pounds ground beef, lean
2 cups shredded cabbage
¼ cup red onion, chopped
Pinch of chopped thyme
3 tablespoons mayonnaise
2 tablespoons orange juice or lime juice (lime juice needs a teaspoon of sugar added)
1 teaspoon of grated orange or lime zest
Salt and freshly ground black pepper to taste

Using a food processor, put the vinegar, water, chili, green onion, garlic, thyme, allspice, cinnamon, nutmeg, ginger, molasses, 1/2 teaspoon each of salt and pepper. Chop finely. If you do not have a food processor, finely mince the chili, garlic, and green onion. Mix ingredients together in a bowl.

Using your hands, gently mix the jerk mixture in with the ground beef in a large bowl until just mixed. Do not over-mix. Shape into patties, about 1/2 inch thick and wider than the diameter of your hamburger bun. Chill about 30 minutes or until you are ready to cook. Note: With jerk seasoning, wash hands with soap and water after handling.

In a medium bowl, gently mix the cabbage, red onion, thyme, mayonnaise, citrus juice, zest, salt and pepper.

Prepare BBQ grill for cooking over high direct heat. Grill the burgers for about 5 minutes per side. Do not press down on the burgers while cooking. Inside cooking, use a grill pan or a cast iron frying pan.

Serve burgers topped with coleslaw, with or without hamburger buns.

Makes 6 burgers.

~°~°~°~°~°~°~°~°~°~°~°~°~°~°

*"As long as you live, keep learning
how to live."—Seneca*

Franks and Sauerkraut Paprikash

1½ pound frankfurters, mild German or Polish sausage or Kielbasa, cut into 2½ inch segments
2 tablespoons butter
2 cups onions, chopped
1 clove garlic, minced
2 teaspoons paprika
1 teaspoon dried dill, or 1 tablespoon fresh chopped dill
1 teaspoon caraway seed
1 cup beef broth or chicken broth
1 large (25-28 ounces) can sauerkraut, drained
2 cups sour cream
   Note: If cooking gluten-free, use gluten-free stock or broth.

Heat a large thick-bottomed pan or Dutch oven on medium heat. Melt the butter, add the onion, garlic, and paprika, cook until the onion is soft, about 5 minutes.

Add the franks, dill, caraway, and broth. Bring to a boil, reduce heat and simmer for 15 minutes.

Add the sauerkraut, simmer, covered, 15 minutes longer.

Remove from heat, stir in the sour cream (do not let the mixture boil after adding the sour cream).

Serves 8. Serve plain, or with boiled or mashed potatoes.

~°~°~°~°~°~°~°~°~°~°~°~°~°~°

Sweet Potato Gnocchi

A new and yummy twist to Gnocchi . . . pair this up with butter or Alfredo sauce. This recipe can be made with butternut squash instead of sweet potatoes.

2 (8 ounces) sweet potatoes
1 clove garlic, pressed
½ teaspoon salt
½ teaspoon ground nutmeg
1 egg
2 cups all-purpose flour

Preheat the oven to 350 °F (175 °C). Bake sweet potatoes for 30 minutes, or until soft to the touch. Remove from the oven, and set aside to cool.

Once the potatoes are cool enough to work with, remove the peels, and mash them, or press them through a ricer into a large bowl. Blend in the garlic, salt, nutmeg, and egg. Mix in the flour a little at a time until you have soft dough. Use more or less flour as needed.

Bring a large pot of lightly salted water to a boil. While you wait for the water, make the gnocchi. On a floured surface, roll the dough out in several long snakes, and cut into 1-inch sections. Drop the pieces into the boiling water, and allow them to cook until they float to the surface. Remove the floating pieces with a slotted spoon, and keep warm in a serving dish. Serve with butter or cream sauce.

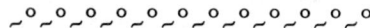

Gnocchi

6 russet potatoes
1 cup all-purpose flour
1 egg, lightly beaten
1 tablespoon olive oil
1 pinch salt

Bring a large pot of salted water to a boil. Drop in potatoes and cook until tender but still firm, about 15 minutes. Drain, cool slightly, and peel. Season with salt, then mash potatoes with fork, masher, or in ricer. Place in large bowl, and stir in egg and olive oil. Knead in enough flour to make a soft dough.

On a floured surface, roll dough into a long rope. Cut the rope into ½ inch pieces.

Bring a large pot of lightly salted water to a boil. Drop in gnocchi, and cook until they float to the top, about 3-5 minutes. Serve with pasta sauce.

~°~°~°~°~°~°~°~°~°~°~°

Alfredo Sauce

3 tablespoons butter
8 fluid ounces heavy whipping cream salt to taste pinch of ground nutmeg
¼ cup Parmesan cheese, grated
¼ cup Romano cheese, grated
1 egg yolk
2 tablespoons Parmesan cheese, grated

Melt butter or margarine in a saucepan over medium heat. Add heavy cream, stirring constantly. Stir in salt, nutmeg, Parmesan cheese, and Romano cheese. Stir constantly until melted, mix in egg yolk. Simmer over medium low heat for 3-5 minutes. Garnish with additional grated Parmesan cheese, if desired.

~°~°~°~°~°~°~°~°~°~°~°

Italian Style Pork Chops

3 cups crushed saltine crackers
2 cups grated Parmesan cheese
1 tablespoon Italian-style seasoning
¼ teaspoon garlic powder
1 cup butter, melted
6 pork chops

Preheat oven to 425 °F (220 °C).

In a medium bowl, combine the crushed saltines, Parmesan cheese, Italian-style seasoning and garlic powder and mix together well.

Dip the chops in the melted butter and then dredge each chop in the cracker mixture, coating all sides thoroughly. Place the chops in a 9 x 13 inch baking dish.

Bake at 425 °F (220 °C) for 30 to 40 minutes, or until internal pork temperature reaches 160 °F (70 °C).

˷°˷°˷°˷°˷°˷°˷°˷°˷°˷°˷°˷°˷°

Foreign Devil Fried Rice

6 sticks dried bean curd
1 tablespoon shredded black fungus
7 dried black mushrooms boiling water
3 1/4 cups water
2 cups basmati rice
1 tablespoon butter or oil
4 eggs, beaten
3 tablespoons vegetable oil, or as needed
1 cup cubed carrots
1 cup chopped yellow onion
4 tablespoons minced fresh ginger root
4 tablespoons minced garlic

½ cup thinly sliced green onions
1 cup frozen peas
3 tablespoons Tamari
2 tablespoons sesame oil fresh ground black pepper

Place the dried bean curd in a bowl, and cover with boiling water. In a smaller bowl, place the shredded black fungus and dried black mushrooms, and cover with boiling water. Allow the bean curd, black fungus, and dried black mushrooms to soak until rehydrated, about 20 minutes.

Place 3 1/4 cups of water with rice in a saucepan. Bring to a boil over high heat, and let it boil hard for one minute. Cover with a lid, and turn heat to low. Cook on low for 5 minutes, then remove from heat (without lifting the lid). Let sit, covered, while you prepare the rest of the meal, or about 20 minutes. Do not at any time lift the lid.

In a non-stick skillet, melt butter over medium-high heat. Scramble eggs to the dry instead of the creamy point. Dump them into a bowl, and continue to chop them into bits with the edge of a wooden spoon. Don't pulverize them, go for pieces about the size of a thumbnail.

In one bowl, combine carrot, onion, garlic, and ginger. In another bowl, green onions and frozen peas. Now drain all the water off the bean curd, fungus and mushrooms. The bean curd might need some tough bits removed, and the remainder cut into quarter-inch rings. The mushrooms only need slicing and the fungus is pre-sliced so no worries there. Combine bean curd and mushrooms in a third bowl.

Heat wok over high heat; let the metal get smoking hot, about one minute. Add three tablespoons of vegetable oil. Wait about 30 seconds, and tip in the bowl of carrot, onion, garlic, and ginger. Cook, stirring frequently. The garlic's going to brown first because it has the highest sugar content, so keep an eye on it, and turn the flame down if necessary. Tip in the bean curd, shredded fungus, and mushrooms, and cook and stir for one minute. Now look to see that your flame is set to maximum, and tip in the spring onion and the frozen peas. You don't need to cook them, just threaten them. Keep them moving, and mix in the rice. Stir in the eggs, and then season with generous, generous amounts of Tamari and sesame oil, and a few twists of fresh black pepper.

~°~°~°~°~°~°~°~°~°~°~°~°~°~°

Note: Fungi used in cooking include black fungus, also known as wood fungus or cloud ears.

<u>MY SPECIAL RECIPES</u>

<u>Wild Game</u>

"Life is like an onion: You peel it off one layer at a time, and sometimes you weep."—Carl Sandburg

Hint:
<u>How to Make Homemade Sausage</u>

Sweet Italian Sausage
4 pounds pork shoulder
1 pound pork fat
40 grams kosher salt
35 grams sugar
20 grams toasted fennel seeds
6 grams cracked black pepper
4 grams ground nutmeg
1 cup minced fresh parsley
1 head garlic, peeled and chopped
¾ cup dry sherry
¼ cup sherry vinegar

Special Equipment Needed for basic sausage:
Meat grinder with coarse and fine dies—either KitchenAid with grinder attachment, a stand-alone grinder, or an old fashioned hand-cranked meat grinder
Additional Equipment Needed for Stuffed Sausage Links:
Casings—hog casings
Sausage stuffer
Wooden rack to hang sausages to dry

MAKING BULK SAUSAGE

Make sure your ingredients are laid out, and the meat and fat are very cold (fat can be completely frozen), before you begin (put meat and fat in freezer for 2 hours). Put bowls and grinder in freezer or refrigerator for an hour before using them.

Prepare a large bowl of ice and put a medium metal bowl on top of it. Slice your meat and fat into chunks between an inch and two inches across. Cut your fat a little smaller than your meat. To keep your ingredients cold, put your cut meat and fat into the bowl set into a larger bowl filled with ice.

When the meat and fat are cut, mix them quickly. Pour in most of your spices; I leave out a tablespoon or two of fennel seeds and a tablespoon of black pepper for later. Mix quickly. Add the salt and the sugar and mix one more time. Put into a covered container or top the bowl with plastic wrap and put the sausage mixture into the freezer for at least 30 minutes and no more than an hour. Now you can call back whoever might have bothered you when you started this process.

Meanwhile, mix ¼ cup of sherry vinegar and ¾ cup of dry sherry and put it in the fridge. I know sherry is not traditional in Italian sausage. You can use white wine and white wine vinegar if you'd rather (I save red wine and red wine vinegar for the hot sausages).

If you plan on stuffing your sausage, take out some of the casings (you need about 15-18 feet for a 5-pound batch of links) and immerse them in warm water. (If you are not planning on stuffing your sausage, you can skip this step.)

After your sausage mixture has chilled, remove your grinder from the freezer and set it up. I use the coarse die for Italian sausage, but you could use either. Do not use a very fine die, because to do this properly you typically need to grind the meat coarse first, then re-chill it, then grind again with the fine die. Besides, an Italian sausage is supposed to be rustic.

Push the sausage mixture though the grinder, working quickly. If you use the KitchenAid attachment, use it on level 4. Make sure the ground meat falls into a cold bowl. When all the meat is ground, put it back in the freezer and clean up the grinder and work area.

When you've cleaned up, take the mixture back out and add the remaining spices and the sherry-sherry vinegar mixture. Using the paddle attachment to a stand mixer (or a stout wooden spoon, or your VERY clean hands), mix the sausage well. With a stand mixer set on level 1, let this go for 90 seconds. It might take a little longer with the spoon or hands. You want the mixture to get a little sticky and begin to bind to itself—it is a lot like what happens when you knead bread.

When this is done, you have sausage. You are done if you are not making links. To cook, take a scoop and form into a ball with your hands. Flatten out a bit. Cook on medium low heat in a skillet for 5-10 minutes each side until browned and cooked through.

Additional STEPS FOR MAKING LINKS

If you are making links, put the mixture back in the freezer and clean up again. Bring out your sausage stuffer, which should have been in the freezer or refrigerator. Run warm water through your sausage casings. This makes them easier to put on the stuffer tube and lets you know if there are any holes in the casings. Be sure to lay one edge of the flushed casings over the edge of the bowl of warm water they were in; this helps you grab them easily when you need them.

Slip a casing onto the stuffing tube (And yes, it is exactly like what you think it is). Leave a "tail" of at least 6 inches off the end of the tube: You need this to tie off later.

Take the meat from the freezer one last time and stuff it into the stuffer. If all the meat will not fit, keep it in a bowl over another bowl filled with ice, or in the fridge while you stuff in batches. Start cranking the stuffer down. Air should be the first thing that emerges—this is why you do not tie off the casing right off the bat.

When the meat starts to come out, use one hand to regulate how fast the casing slips off the tube; it's a little tricky at first, but you will get the hang of it. Let the sausage come out in one long coil; you will make links later. Remember to leave 6-10 inches of "tail" at the other end of the casing. Sometimes one really long hog casing is all you need for a 5-pound batch. When the sausage is all in the casings, tie off the one end in a double knot. You could also use fine butcher's twine.

With two hands, pinch off what will become two links. Work the links so they are pretty tight: You want any air bubbles to force their way to the edge of the sausage. Then spin the link you have between your fingers away from you several times. Repeat this process down the coil, only on this next link, spin it towards you several times. Continue this way, alternating, until you get to the end of the coil. Tie off the other end.

Almost done. Time to hang your sausages. Hang them on the rack so they don't touch (too much), and find yourself a needle. Sterilize the needle, then look for air bubbles in the links. Prick them with the needle, and in most cases the casing will flatten itself against the link.

Let these dry for an hour or two, then put them in a large container in the fridge overnight, with paper towels underneath. Package them up or eat them the next day. They will keep for a week, but freeze those that will not be used by then.

Makes 5 lbs of sausage, or about 15-20 links.

Note: Same principle for any meat just the ingredients change

_° _° _° _° _° _° _° _° _° _° _° _° _° _°

Stuffed Rolled Venison Log

2 pounds ground venison
1 medium onion, chopped
1½ cups Quaker Oats (uncooked)
4 tablespoons A-1 Sauce
8 slices boiled deli ham
1 pound shredded mozzarella cheese
Salt and pepper to taste

Mix venison, onion, oats, A-1, salt, and pepper. Shape into a loaf.

Spread aluminum foil on a flat surface and flatten loaf to approximately 12 x 14 x ½ inch thick. Lay slices of ham on top to cover entire surface. Cover with mozzarella cheese. Roll up and pinch sides.

Bake @ 350 °F. for one hour covered with foil. Remove foil and cook venison meatloaf an additional 30 minutes until brown on top.

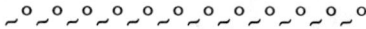

Slow Cooker Venison Roast

3 pounds boneless venison roast
1 large onion, sliced
1 tablespoon soy sauce
1 tablespoon Worcestershire sauce
1 tablespoon garlic salt
1/4 teaspoon ground black pepper
1 (1 ounce) package dry onion soup mix
1 (10.75 ounces) can condensed cream of mushroom soup

Put cleaned meat in slow cooker and cover with onion. Sprinkle with soy sauce, Worcestershire sauce, garlic salt and pepper.

In a small bowl combine the soup mix and the soup; mix together and pour mixture over venison. Cook on Low setting for 6 hours.

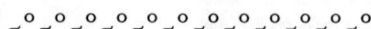

Slow Cooker Moose Roast

2 tablespoons vegetable oil
4 pounds moose roast
2 cups apple juice
1 (1 ounce) envelope dry onion soup mix

Heat oil in a large skillet over medium-high heat. Brown the roast on all sides in the hot oil. Remove, and transfer to a slow cooker.

Sprinkle onion soup mix over the roast, then pour in the apple juice. Cover and cook on MEDIUM for 6 to 8 hours, or until meat is very tender. Check occasionally to make sure there is sufficient liquid, and add more juice if necessary. Serve roast with juices, or thicken them for tasty gravy.

Peppered Elk Skillet

1 tablespoon vegetable oil
1 pound elk steak, cut into thin strips
1 clove minced garlic salt and pepper to taste
1 tablespoon vegetable oil
2 green bell peppers, cut into strips

1 medium onion, chopped
1 cup beef broth
1 tablespoon soy sauce
1 (14.5 ounces) can diced tomatoes
1 (8 ounces) package sliced mushrooms
1 (15 ounces) can baby corn, drained
1½ tablespoons cornstarch
¼ cup water

Heat 1 tablespoon of oil in a large skillet over medium-high heat. Add the elk strips and garlic; cook and stir until the elk has browned, about 4 minutes. Once done, season to taste with salt and pepper, and remove elk from skillet.

Pour the remaining tablespoon of oil into the skillet, and stir in bell pepper and onion. Cook and stir until the vegetables are tender, about 5 minutes, then add the beef broth, soy sauce, tomatoes, mushrooms, and corn. Bring to a boil. Dissolve cornstarch in water, and stir into boiling vegetables; stir until thickened, about 30 seconds. Stir in the browned elk until heated through, then serve.

Sweet and Sour Elk

1 envelope onion soup mix
¼ cup water
1 (12 ounces) jar apricot preserves
½ cup Russian or Catalina salad dressing
¼ cup packed brown sugar
1 tablespoon cider vinegar
1½ pounds elk steaks, cut into ½ inch strips
1 teaspoon salt
¼ teaspoon pepper
Hot cooked rice

RJ Woodward

In a bowl, combine soup mix and water; let stand for 15 minutes. Add preserves, salad dressing, brown sugar and vinegar; mix well. Place elk in a greased 13 x 9 x 2 inches baking dish. Sprinkle with salt and pepper. Pour apricot mixture over the elk. Cover and bake @ 350 °F for 45 minutes. Uncover and bake 30-40 minutes longer or until meat is fork-tender. Serve over rice.

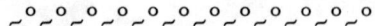

<u>MY SPECIAL RECIPES</u>

Chapter Four

Soups, Salads
and Vegetables

"There is no love sincerer than the love of food."
—*George Bernard Shaw*

Hint:
Cooking Pumpkin Seeds
Lay the pumpkin seeds relatively flat on a pan.
Spray them with PAM or another cooking oil.
Sprinkle any combination of salt, garlic salt, onion powder, or any other preferred seasoning on top of the pumpkin seeds. Toss the seeds then to coat them with your chosen seasoning.

Put in the toaster oven or regular oven at about 350 °F for about an hour, tossing the seeds every 15-20 minutes.

TIP:
Gettin' Saucy
Classic cheese sauce begins with a béchamel sauce, a simple sauce made of butter, flour, milk, and a few seasonings.
To begin, make a roux:
Measure out equal amounts of butter and flour.

Dice the butter into small cubes and melt it in a saucepan over low heat.

Once the butter is melted, begin whisking in the flour.

When all the flour is incorporated, continue stirring and cooking for a few minutes to activate the starch granules.

If you're making a white or light-coloured cheese sauce, keep the heat low enough so the roux does not brown.

Next comes the milk. If the roux is hot, the milk should be cool, but if the roux is cool, the milk should be hot. Combining the two ingredients at different temperatures ensures that they will heat up at a moderate rate—not too fast, and not too slow—creating a velvety-smooth sauce.

Whisk the mixture until smooth, then add seasonings if you wish. Traditional seasonings for béchamel are diced onion, a bay leaf, a couple cloves, and a pinch of nutmeg.

Allow the sauce to simmer until it has lost its "floury" taste (about 20 minutes), then strain out any seasonings.

Remove the pan from the heat and gently blend in the cheese. If the cheese doesn't seem to be melting, return the pan to very low heat, but watch it carefully and remove as soon as the cheese is melted.

Béchamel Sauce:
4 tablespoons butter
2 tablespoons grated onion
2 tablespoons all-purpose flour
1 cup chicken broth
1 cup half-and-half
1/2 teaspoon salt
1/4 teaspoon ground white pepper
1 pinch dried thyme
1 pinch ground cayenne pepper

MICROWAVE METHOD: In microwave oven, melt butter in a 1-quart glass measuring pitcher for about 1 minute at HIGH.

Add grated onion and flour and mix well. Gradually add warm or room temperature chicken broth (NOT hot) and half-and-half to container, stirring constantly.

Cook uncovered for 5-6 minutes at HIGH or until sauce is thickened. Do NOT boil.

After 2 minutes, stir mixture, then stir again every 30 seconds to one minute as needed. When sauce reaches medium thickness, remove from microwave, add seasonings and stir.

STOVETOP METHOD: In a small saucepan, melt butter and stir in the flour, salt and white pepper. Add cold half-and-half and COLD chicken broth all at once. Stir well. Cook, stirring frequently, at medium heat until thick. Remove from heat and stir in seasoning.

<u>*Four Cheese Sauce:*</u>
2 cups heavy whipping cream
½ cup butter
½ cup grated Parmesan cheese
½ cup shredded mozzarella cheese
½ cup shredded provolone cheese
½ cup grated Romano cheese

In a medium saucepan combine whipping cream and butter. Bring to a simmer over medium heat, stirring frequently until butter melts. Gradually stir in grated Parmesan cheese, grated mozzarella cheese, grated provolone cheese, and grated Romano cheese. Reduce heat to low, and continue to stir just until all cheese is melted.

Serve immediately, sauce will thicken upon standing.

ͺₒ ͺₒ ͺₒ ͺₒ ͺₒ ͺₒ ͺₒ ͺₒ ͺₒ ͺₒ ͺₒ ͺₒ ͺₒ ₒ

Vegetables

"Shipping is a terrible thing to do to vegetables.
They probably get jet-lagged, just like
people."—Elizabeth Berry

TIP:
Cook vegetables with one or more bouillon cubes instead of salt; improves flavour. Tossing in a few garlic cloves when boiling vegetables makes things tastier too.

Lemon juice or vinegar in water where cauliflower is cooked makes it keep its white color.

Picnic Potato Squares

2 packages (7.5 grams each) unflavoured gelatin
2½ cups milk, divided
1 cup mayonnaise
1 tablespoon prepared mustard
2 teaspoons sugar
½ teaspoon salt
Pepper to taste
2½ cups potatoes, cubed, cooked, cooled
½ cup carrot, shredded
½ cup celery, thinly sliced
½ cup dill pickle, chopped
2 tablespoons onion, diced
Lettuce leaves optional

Place the gelatin and 1 cup of milk in a saucepan, let stand for1 minute. Cook over low heat until gelatin is dissolved. Remove from heat, stir in mayonnaise, mustard, sugar, salt, pepper and remaining milk until smooth. Fold in potatoes, carrots, celery, pickles and onions. Pour into ungreased 8 inches square pan. Chill until firm, cut into squares. Serve on lettuce leaves.

ₒ ₀ ₒ ₀ ₒ ₀ ₒ ₀ ₒ ₀ ₒ ₀ ₒ ₀ ₒ ₀ ₒ ₀ ₒ

TIP:

Wrapping celery in aluminum foil when storing it in the refrigerator will help to keep it fresher for weeks.

To keep your potatoes from budding out, place an apple in the bag with the potatoes.

ₒ ₀ ₒ ₀ ₒ ₀ ₒ ₀ ₒ ₀ ₒ ₀ ₒ ₀ ₒ ₀ ₒ ₀ ₒ

<u>Green Beans With Pine Nuts</u>

1 pound green beans, whole
1/3 cup pine nuts, roasted
¼ cup olive oil
¼ cup red wine vinegar
1 tablespoon fresh oregano
2 large red bell peppers, roasted, peeled, cored, seeded and cut into strips
1 garlic clove, minced
1 tablespoon fresh cilantro, chopped
Salt and pepper to taste
¼ cup parmesan cheese, shaved

Cook the beans in boiling water until tender. Drain and rinse with cold water. In a large skillet, stir together the nuts, olive oil, vinegar, oregano, cilantro and garlic. Add the beans and cook, stirring over medium-low heat until all ingredients are heated through. Add salt and pepper, and sprinkle the cheese over all.

ₒ ₀ ₒ ₀ ₒ ₀ ₒ ₀ ₒ ₀ ₒ ₀ ₒ ₀ ₒ ₀ ₒ

Easy Vegetable Pot Pie

1 (10.75 ounces) can condensed cream of potato soup
1 (15 ounces) can mixed vegetables, drained
½ cup milk
½ teaspoon dried thyme
½ teaspoon ground black pepper
2 (9 inch) frozen prepared pie crusts, thawed
1 egg, lightly beaten

Preheat oven to 375 °F (190 °C).

In a medium bowl, combine potato soup, mixed vegetables, milk, thyme, and black pepper.

Spoon filling into bottom pie crust. Cover with top crust, and crimp edges to seal. Slit top crust, and brush with beaten egg if desired.

Bake for 40 minutes. Remove from oven, and cool for 10 minutes before serving

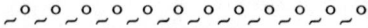

Slow Cooker Vegetarian Chili

1 (19 ounces) can black bean soup
1 (15 ounces) can kidney beans, rinsed and drained
1 (15 ounces) can garbanzo beans, rinsed and drained
1 (16 ounces) can vegetarian baked beans
1 (14.5 ounces) can chopped tomatoes in puree
1 (15 ounces) can whole kernel corn, drained
1 onion, chopped
1 green bell pepper, chopped
2 stalks celery, chopped
2 cloves garlic, chopped
1 tablespoon chili powder, or to taste
1 tablespoon dried parsley

1 tablespoon dried oregano
1 tablespoon dried basil

In a slow cooker, combine black bean soup, kidney beans, garbanzo beans, baked beans, tomatoes, corn, onion, bell pepper and celery. Season with garlic, chili powder, parsley, oregano and basil. Cook for at least two hours on High.

˷°˷°˷°˷°˷°˷°˷°˷°˷°˷°˷°˷°˷°

Poor Man's Caviar

2 large avocados—peeled, pitted, and chopped
3 plum tomatoes, chopped
1 bunch green onions, chopped
1 (14.5 ounces) can black beans, rinsed and drained
1 (11 ounces) can Mexicorn, drained
¼ cup red wine vinegar
¼ cup canola oil hot pepper sauce to taste

Stir together avocados, tomatoes, green onions, black beans, and Mexicorn. Stir in red wine vinegar, canola oil, and hot pepper sauce. Cover, and chill 1 hour. Serve with tortillas chips or pita bread

˷°˷°˷°˷°˷°˷°˷°˷°˷°˷°˷°˷°˷°

Mexicorn

3 (15 ounces) cans black beans, rinsed and drained
3 (15.25 ounces) cans whole kernel corn, drained
1/2 red onion, diced
2 green bell peppers, diced
1 (7 ounces) jar roasted red peppers, drained and diced

1/3 cup red wine vinegar
1/3 cup canola oil

Into a large bowl, mix together the beans, corn, red onion, green pepper and red pepper.

Right before serving, pour enough red wine vinegar over all to coat. Add just enough oil to make it shiny.

~°~°~°~°~°~°~°~°~°~°~°~°~°~°~°

TIP:
Add 1/4 tsp. of baking powder per quart of potatoes while mashing them and they will be fluffy, smooth, and more tasty.

Adding a pinch of sugar to the water when boiling corn on the cob helps bring out the corn's natural sweetness

Roasted Baby Potatoes

3 tablespoons extra-virgin olive oil
1 tablespoon grainy mustard
1 teaspoon kosher salt
½ teaspoon pepper
1 clove garlic, minced
1 tablespoon chopped fresh rosemary, or 1/2 tsp dried
2 pounds baby potatoes, cut in half if necessary
2 shallots, thinly sliced
2 tablespoons chopped fresh parsley

In a large bowl, combine oil, mustard, salt, pepper, garlic and rosemary. Add potatoes and shallots and toss together.

Spread potatoes and shallots on a parchment-lined baking sheet. Bake in a preheated 425°F (220°C) oven for 45 to 60 minutes, or until lightly browned and tender.

Sprinkle with parsley before serving.

~°~°~°~°~°~°~°~°~°~°~°~°~°~°~°

Parisian Potatoes (Pommes Parisienne)

9 potatoes
3 small shallots
3 tablespoons extra virgin olive oil
3 tablespoons butter, melted
1 clove garlic, minced
2 sprigs of thyme, leaves only
1 tablespoons parsley—finely chopped
Salt to taste

Peel the potatoes.
Using a Parisienne scoop (or melon baller), scoop out balls of potato, approximately 1.5cm in diameter.
Place the potato balls in a pot and cover with cold water.
Bring to the boil and then drain, cool
Add the shallots and oil to a large plastic bag put potatoes in the bag and shake.
Place in baking dish, adding melted butter, garlic, thyme, parsley and salt. Bake @ 425°F (220°C) turning often until golden brown

~°~°~°~°~°~°~°~°~°~°~°~°~°~°~°

Baked Stuffed Potatoes with Roasted Garlic
8-10 cloves garlic, split and tipped salt and freshly ground pepper
1 tablespoon plus 2 teaspoons extra-virgin olive oil, plus more for drizzling and brushing
1 ½ pounds baby potatoes (about 18), scrubbed
1/3 cup sour cream
1 teaspoon finely chopped fresh thyme

Preheat oven to 400 °F. Place garlic on parchment-lined foil. Season with salt and pepper, generously drizzle with oil, and wrap. Roast until fragrant and soft, about 1 hour. Leave oven on.

Cover potatoes with salted water in a medium saucepan. Bring to a boil, and cook until fork tender, about 20 minutes. Drain, and return to hot pan. Let stand for 5 minutes to dry.

Halve potatoes crosswise. Trim (and reserve) rounded ends of each half slightly, so potatoes sit flat with cut sides up. Scoop out flesh using a melon baller, leaving a thin layer on bottom and sides, and add contents to a bowl. Peel reserved ends; add to bowl. Stir in oil, sour cream, and thyme. Squeeze split garlic cloves from skins into potato mixture. Mash until smooth. Season with salt and pepper.

Lightly brush a baking sheet with oil. Fill each potato half with about 1 teaspoons potato mixture, mounding slightly. Place potatoes 1 inch apart on sheet, and lightly drizzle with oil. Bake until golden brown, 25-30 minutes.

Bring to room temperature, and bake just before serving.

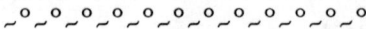

MY SPECIAL RECIPES

<u>Salads</u>

"The art of life is a constant readjustment to our surroundings."
—Kakuzo Okakaura

3 Sherry Vinegar-based Vinaigrettes:

* *Sherry-Shallot Vinaigrette:*
This is a great all-purpose vinaigrette for salads, sliced tomatoes or other raw vegetables.
2 tablespoons sherry vinegar
1 tablespoon minced shallot
Salt and pepper to taste
6 tablespoons vegetable oil

Combine the vinegar, shallot, salt and pepper. Give it a stir with a whisk or fork to soften the shallot then drizzle the oil in while whisking.

* *Tarragon-Mustard Vinaigrette:*
This is a little heartier than the above, can be used to dress greens, whole vegetables and would make a lovely sauce drizzled over lean white fish.
2 tablespoons sherry vinegar
1 tablespoon minced shallot
Salt and pepper to taste
6 tablespoons vegetable oil

1-2 teaspoons whole grain or Dijon mustard
1 tablespoon minced tarragon

Combine the vinegar, shallot, salt, pepper, and mustard. Give it a stir with a whisk or fork to soften the shallot then drizzle the oil in while whisking. Stir in the tarragon just before serving.

❖ *Gribiche Vinaigrette:*
Gribiche is traditionally mayonnaise based, but I like it as a vinaigrette better. It makes a wonderful sauce for roasted pork loin, or any pork preparation.
2 tablespoons sherry vinegar
1 tablespoon minced shallot
Salt and pepper to taste
1 teaspoon whole grain or Dijon mustard
6 tablespoons vegetable oil
1 tablespoon minced tarragon
1 hard cooked egg, finely chopped
1 tablespoon chopped cornichons
2 teaspoons capers, roughly chopped

Combine the vinegar, shallot, salt, pepper, and mustard. Give it a stir with a whisk or fork to soften the shallot then drizzle the oil in while whisking. Stir in the tarragon, egg, cornichons and capers.

~°~°~°~°~°~°~°~°~°~°~°~°~°~°

Black Bean Salad

1 (15 ounces) can of black beans, thoroughly rinsed, and drained (or 1½ cups of freshly cooked black beans)

1½ cups frozen corn, defrosted (or fresh corn, parboiled, drained and cooled)

½ cup chopped green onions or shallots

2 fresh jalapeño peppers, seeded and minced, or 1 whole pickled jalapeño pepper, minced (not seeded)

3 fresh plum tomatoes, seeded and chopped

1 avocado, peeled, seeded, and cut into chunks

½ cup fresh cilantro, chopped

¼ cup fresh basil, chopped

2 tablespoons lime juice (about the amount of juice from one lime)

1 tablespoon olive oil

½-1 teaspoon of sugar (to taste)

Salt and pepper to taste

Make sure to rinse and drain the beans, if you are using canned beans.

In a large bowl, combine the beans, corn, onions, jalapeno chili peppers, tomatoes, avocado, cilantro, basil, lime juice and olive oil. Add sugar and salt and pepper to taste. (The sugar will help balance the acidity from the tomatoes and lime juice.) Chill before serving.

Serves 6 to 8.

Smoked Salmon Pasta Salad

This recipe can easily be halved or doubled.

1 pound of dry penne rigati, gemelli, fusilli, or other short-cut pasta, or a combination

Salt for the pasta water

Olive oil

1-2 tablespoons mayonnaise

4 ounce smoked salmon, shredded

½ cup orange or yellow bell pepper, finely chopped

½ cup celery, finely chopped

¼ cup green onions (scallions), chopped

1 teaspoon salt
Freshly ground pepper
Pinch dried dill
1 tablespoon lemon juice

Bring a large pot of salted water to a boil (use a tablespoon of salt for every 2 quarts of water). Add the pasta. Cook uncovered, at a rolling boil until al dente, or tender, but still a bit firm. Drain and rinse under cold water. (If you are making the pasta ahead of time, stir in a little olive oil to keep the pasta from sticking to each other.) Note that if you are using different kinds of pasta, you may want to cook them separately as different types of pasta cook at different rates.

Stir in the rest of the ingredients, adjusting the amounts of mayonnaise, lemon juice, salt, and pepper to taste.

Serve chilled or at room temperature.

Serves 8.

Grilled Corn Salad

4 ears of corn, do not shuck (or 2½ cups frozen corn for the non-grill option)
1 large red bell pepper
1 zucchini, sliced in half lengthwise
½ cup red onion, chopped
½ cup cilantro, chopped
1 chili pepper, seeded and minced (optional)
1 teaspoon ground cumin
¼ cup crumbly salty cheese such as feta or cotija (optional)
2 tablespoons olive oil
2 tablespoons cider vinegar or lime juice
Salt and freshly ground pepper to taste

Prepare your BBQ grill for high, direct heat. Oil the grill grates. Rub a little olive oil over the bell pepper. Place the corn (in their husks) and red bell pepper directly on the grill grates. Cover the grill.

Turn corn occasionally, so that every part of the husk is blackened. Turn the red bell pepper occasionally until the skin has blistered up all around it. This should take 15-20 minutes.

For the last 5 minutes or so, rub olive oil over the zucchini pieces and place the zucchini pieces directly on the grill grate, cut side down. Turn them over after a few minutes when they have some nice grill marks on them. Let them cook for just a minute or two on the other side.

Let the corn cool down for a few minutes and pull back the husks. Stand the corn husks vertically, tip facing down, in a large shallow bowl or baking dish. Use a sharp knife to make long, downward strokes, removing the kernels from the cob, as you work your way around the cob.

Once the bell pepper has cooled a bit, remove the outer peel. Cut open the pepper, remove the seeds and stem. Chop the bell pepper into small pieces.

Slice the slightly browned zucchini again lengthwise and chop into small pieces.

Alternative—no grill version: Alternatively you can prepare the vegetables on the stove-top. Shuck the corn and use a knife to remove the kernels from the cobs. If you don't have fresh corn, you can easily use frozen. Coat the bottom of a large, sturdy relatively stick-free (can use cast iron) pan with a little olive oil. Heat the pan to high. Spread out the corn kernels on the pan. If frozen, they will defrost almost immediately. Don't stir them that much, just let them cook, stirring occasionally, until they start to toast. When they get a little browned, remove them from the pan to a bowl. Lay the zucchini pieces on the pan and brown on both sides, do not over cook, remove from pan. The bell pepper does not need to be cooked, it can just be seeded and chopped fine.

Place grilled or toasted corn kernels, chopped bell pepper, chopped zucchini, red onion, cilantro, and chili pepper into a large bowl. Add the cumin, olive oil, vinegar or lime juice, and crumbly cheese. Mix gently. Salt and pepper to taste.

Serve cold or at room temperature. Serves 4.

*"Cheese—milk's leap toward immortality.
"—Clifton Fadiman*

Salad Dressings:

Blue Cheese Dressing
1 cup mayonnaise
1 cup sour cream
1 cup buttermilk
4 ounces blue cheese, crumbled
1 tablespoon hot pepper sauce
1 teaspoon garlic powder
1 tablespoon Worcestershire sauce
2 tablespoons grated Parmesan cheese
1 tablespoon dried parsley

Whisk together the mayonnaise, sour cream, buttermilk, hot sauce, garlic powder, Worcestershire sauce, parmesan cheese and parsley flakes. Add blue cheese, mix and refrigerate until chilled.

Lemon Dill Salad Dressing
2 cups mayonnaise
½ cup lemon juice
¼ cup dried dill weed to taste
½ cup buttermilk

In a medium bowl, whisk together the mayonnaise, lemon juice, dill and buttermilk. Chill until serving.

～°～°～°～°～°～°～°～°～°～°～°～°～°

Russian Salad Dressing
½ cup mayonnaise
1/3 cup ketchup
1 tablespoon red wine vinegar
1 tablespoon finely chopped onion salt and pepper to taste

In a small bowl, whisk together the mayonnaise, ketchup, vinegar, onion, salt and pepper until thoroughly combined. Refrigerate until ready to use.

～°～°～°～°～°～°～°～°～°～°～°～°～°

Thousand Island Dressing
3 eggs
¼ cup Worcestershire sauce
1 tablespoon white sugar
¼ cup white vinegar
1 pinch ground cloves
1 quart mayonnaise
¾ cup sweet pickle relish
½ cup chopped black olives
½ cup diced red bell pepper

Place eggs in a saucepan and cover with cold water. Bring water to a boil and immediately remove from heat. Cover and let eggs stand in hot water for 10-12 minutes. Remove from hot water, cool, peel and chop.

In a medium bowl, whisk together the chopped eggs, Worcestershire sauce, sugar, vinegar, cloves, mayonnaise, relish, olives and red pepper until evenly blended. Chill and serve spooned over fresh greens. Store in the refrigerator.

~°~°~°~°~°~°~°~°~°~°~°~°~°~°

Spicy Ranch Dressing
1 cup mayonnaise
1 cup buttermilk
3 tablespoons dry ranch salad dressing mix
2 tablespoons finely chopped red bell pepper
1 tablespoon chopped fresh cilantro
1 small jalapeno pepper, seeded and coarsely chopped
1 dash hot pepper sauce (e.g. Tabasco™), or to taste

In a blender, combine the mayonnaise, buttermilk, ranch dressing mix, bell pepper, cilantro, jalapeno pepper and hot pepper sauce. Pulse until blended.

~°~°~°~°~°~°~°~°~°~°~°~°~°~°

Snappy Balsamic Dressing
½ cup balsamic vinegar
½ cup olive oil
2 cloves garlic, pressed
2 teaspoons crushed fennel seed
½ teaspoon salt
1 teaspoon pepper

In a jar with a tight fitting lid, or cruet with a stopper, combine the balsamic vinegar, olive oil, garlic, fennel seed, salt and pepper. Seal, and shake vigorously to mix. Shake again just before serving.

~°~°~°~°~°~°~°~°~°~°~°~°~°~°

<u>*Simple Caesar Salad Dressing*</u>
1/3 cup lemon juice
1/3 cup white vinegar
1/3 cup water
¼ cup shredded Parmesan cheese
2½ tablespoons prepared Dijon-style mustard
1 teaspoon garlic powder
¼ teaspoon ground black pepper

In a jar with a lid, combine lemon juice, vinegar, water, cheese, mustard, garlic powder and pepper. Cover and shake well. Refrigerate until ready to use.

꘏°꘏°꘏°꘏°꘏°꘏°꘏°꘏°꘏°꘏°꘏°꘏°꘏°꘏°

<u>*Pepper-Parmesan Dressing*</u>
½ cup sour cream
¾ cup low fat buttermilk
½ cup grated Parmesan cheese
2 cloves garlic, minced
6 tablespoons white wine vinegar
1½ tablespoons freshly ground black pepper
2 pinches salt

Place sour cream, buttermilk, Parmesan, garlic, vinegar, pepper and salt into a blender or food processor and blend until well combined. Transfer to a container with a tight-fitting lid and refrigerate for at least one hour for best flavour.

Note: Adjust amounts of salt and pepper to taste. If a thinner consistency is desired, add more buttermilk. To thicken, add equal parts of sour cream and parmesan. Ideal for dipping veggies.

꘏°꘏°꘏°꘏°꘏°꘏°꘏°꘏°꘏°꘏°꘏°꘏°꘏°꘏°

Roquefort Dressing
2 cups mayonnaise
1½ cups buttermilk
8 ounces Roquefort cheese, crumbled
2 tablespoons Worcestershire sauce
1 teaspoon garlic powder

In a blender or food processor, combine mayonnaise, buttermilk, cheese, Worcestershire and garlic powder, and process until smooth. Store in tightly covered jar in the refrigerator until ready to serve. Serve over tossed salad greens.

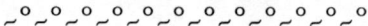

Cole Slaw Dressing
1¼ cup mayonnaise
1/3 cup sugar
¼ cup cider vinegar
¼ teaspoon celery seed
½ teaspoon Creole seasoning or seasoned salt
½ teaspoon horseradish, finely minced
¼ teaspoon black pepper salt, to taste

Combine all ingredients in a jar; shake well. Refrigerate for about an hour; dress shredded cabbage. This makes enough for about 1 medium head of cabbage. I add a little grated carrot and onion to the mixture, or you could use green cabbage with a little red cabbage.

"Life's a tough proposition, and the first hundred
years are the hardest."
—Wilson Mizner

TIP:
*If you scorch milk by accident, put the pan in cold water and
add a pinch of salt. Takes away the burned taste.*

*Try freezing half and half or other cream in an ice cube tray and
then store the cubes in a Ziploc bag in the freezer. Then when you
make something like a soup or sauce, you can just take out a cube or
two. This works great if you live alone too and never need a big batch
of anything. These cubes can be used to add flavour to anything!*

Broccoli Salad

1 cup cheddar cheese, grated
2 bunches broccoli
4 green onions, chopped
½ pound bacon, cooked and crumbled
½ cup frozen peas
4 boiled eggs, chopped
½ cup white vinegar
3-4 tablespoons mayonnaise

Chop broccoli into bite-sized pieces. Add onions, crumbled
bacon, peas, eggs and cheese to broccoli.

Mix together mayonnaise, vinegar and sugar; pour over
vegetable mixture.

Jellied Pineapple and Carrot Salad

1 package lemon jello
1 cup boiling water
1 tablespoon vinegar
1 cup pineapple juice
½ teaspoon salt
1 cup crushed pineapple, drained
1 cup carrots, grated or shredded

Dissolve jello in boiling water. Add pineapple juice, vinegar and salt. Chill until slightly thickened. Add pineapple and raw carrot. Pour into a mould and chill until firm.

Ambrosia

2 cups sour cream
1 (14 ounces) can pineapple tidbits, drained
1 small package white mini marshmallows
1 (14 ounces) can peaches, sliced, drained
1 small jar maraschino cherries, rinsed, drained
Mix together well and leave covered in fridge for at least 4 hours.

Other variations include coloured marshmallows, mandarin oranges and coconut.

Nutty Quinoa Salad

1 cup quinoa
2 cups water
2 teaspoons orange rind, grated
½ cup raisins
¼ cup canola oil
3 green onions
½ cup peanuts
Mint leaves
Shredded carrots, celery, red peppers

Combine quinoa and water in large saucepan; bring to boil. Reduce heat, cover and simmer for 10 minutes. Add raisins and continue cooking until all liquid has evaporated. Remove from heat.

Spread on baking sheet and let cool completely

In large bowl combine all ingredients. Toss. Serve with cold cuts.

~°~°~°~°~°~°~°~°~°~°~°~°~°~°

Wheat Salad

1 cup wheat
1 (8 ounces) package cream cheese
2 packages vanilla instant pudding
1 large container Cool Whip
1 large can pineapple, crushed, drained

Soak wheat overnight. Cook slowly for 2-3 hours in a good sized pot. Drain wheat and let cool.

Add cream cheese, vanilla instant pudding, Cool Whip and pineapple. Beat everything together and add wheat. Refrigerate.

~°~°~°~°~°~°~°~°~°~°~°~°~°~°

24 Hour Cole Slaw

1 large head cabbage, shredded
1 medium or green onions
2 small carrots, shredded
1 green pepper, diced (optional)
Dressing: 1 cup vinegar
1 teaspoon salt
1 teaspoon dry mustard
¾ cup white sugar
2/3 cup salad oil
    Dressing: Heat all ingredients to a boil.
    Pour hot syrup over vegetables. Mix well. Seal in jars. Store in fridge.

~°~°~°~°~°~°~°~°~°~°~°~°~°~°

Cucumber Salad

2 large English cucumbers, seeds removed, coarsely grated
1 medium onion, finely diced
1/3 cup mayonnaise
2 tablespoons sour cream
2 tablespoons vinegar
1 tablespoon honey
2 tablespoons poppy seeds or to taste
Salt and pepper to taste.

Wash and quarter cucumbers lengthwise, remove seeds. Note: if you leave seeds in the salad gets watery. Coarsely grate remaining cucumber skins on, add diced onion. Mix in remaining ingredients. Cool till time to serve.

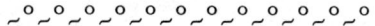

<u>MY SPECIAL RECIPES</u>

<u>Soups</u>

*"If more of us valued food and cheer and song
above hoarded gold, it would be a merrier
world."*
J.R Tolkien

TIPS:
How To Make the Best Soup:
Make soup 1-2 days in advance to let flavors blend.

Reserve the vegetable cooking water and use in place of plain water to improve soup flavour.

Shin, marrow, neck and oxtail bones are best for stock flavouring.

Veal knuckles are best for making jellied stocks.

If soup tastes thin or weak, add bouillon cubes or powder as strengtheners.

Cool soup uncovered as quickly as possible by placing pot in sink of ice water.

Cold soups dull the taste buds and usually need more seasonings than hot soup. Taste and adjust before serving.

If using beer or wine in the soup, reduce salt slightly.

Wine added to soups should be done shortly before serving and do not let it boil.

Too much wine will make soup bitter. 1/4-1/3 cup per quart is plenty.

When reducing or boiling down a soup stock, do not add salt until the end.

If soup is too salty, add half a peeled raw potato and simmer about 15 minutes to absorb excess salt and then remove potato.

1 teaspoon of sugar or light brown sugar will mellow the acidity of tomato soup.

Vegetable cream soups can be thickened by pureeing some of the vegetables with a bit of the liquid.

Add herbs at the end to preserve the most flavour.

Never boil a chowder.

Hints:

As a general rule, 1 quart soup equals 6 first-course servings or 3-4 main course servings.

Use a soup tureen when serving soup as a main course to lend elegance to the table and keep soup hot for seconds.

Match a light-flavoured soup to a rich or spicy main dish and vice versa.

<u>*Basic Needs:*</u> *soup or stew pot, or*

Dutch oven, or

Crock pot meat bones for stock vegetables herbs

Making Chicken Stock

Chicken stock is used as the base for many soups and sauces, as well as adding flavour and richness to rice dishes, stews, and pastas.

To make basic chicken stock: bones from two chickens, water

2 medium onions
2 medium carrots
2 stalks celery
12+ whole black peppercorns
1 bay leaf

This yields about 2 quarts of stock.

Remove as much fat from the chicken bones as possible.

Place the bones in a large stockpot and add water to cover. Bring the water to a near-boil, and immediately reduce the heat to low.

Note: Boiling causes impurities to churn in the pot rather than rise to the top where you can skim off any foam.

Cooking at a low simmer ensures a clear golden stock.

While the water is heating, chop the vegetables. Quarter the onions or cut them in large chunks.

Peel and trim the ends off the carrots. Cut them in thirds or coarsely chop.

You can add the entire celery stalk, leaves and all—just be sure to clean the leaves thoroughly. Cut the celery into chunks.

Combine the chopped veggies, peppercorns, and bay leaf in a bowl.

Check the simmering stock: a layer of fat will have risen to the surface.

Use a ladle or skimmer to strain off the fat.

After the stock has simmered for about 1 hour and 15 minutes, add the vegetables to the pot. Bring the stock back to a simmer and cook for an additional 45 minutes, skimming occasionally if fat rises to the surface.

Strain the stock through a fine colander. Discard vegetables, bay leaf and peppercorns.

The finished stock should be a clear, light tan color and have little or no fat floating on the surface. The stock is now ready to use. If you don't need the full amount for soup, pour it into ice cube trays and freeze them. Then you'll have small amounts ready to use when making a sauce, gravy, mashed potatoes, casseroles, or rice dishes.

> *"We make a living by what we get, but we make*
> *a life by what we give."*
> *—Winston Churchill*

Black Bean and Corn Soup

1 tablespoon olive oil
1 large onion, chopped
1 stalk celery, chopped
2 carrots, chopped
4 cloves garlic, chopped
2 tablespoons chili powder
1 tablespoon ground cumin

Black pepper to taste
4 cups organic vegetable broth
4 (15 ounces) cans black beans
8 ounces frozen corn
1 (14.5 ounces) can tomatoes, crushed

Heat oil in a large pot over medium-high heat. Sauté onions, celery, carrots and garlic for 5 minutes. Season with chili powder, cumin and black pepper; cook for 1 minute. Stir in vegetable broth, 2 cans of beans and corn. Bring to boil. Process remaining 2 can beans and tomatoes in a food processor until smooth. Stir into boiling soup mixture, reduce heat and simmer for 15 minutes.

~°~°~°~°~°~°~°~°~°~°~°~°~°~°

Chicken and Corn Chowder

5 slices bacon
12 ounces fully cooked grilled chicken breasts, cut into cubes
½ cup onion, chopped
½ cup sweet bell pepper, chopped
1 clove garlic, minced
4 cups chicken broth
1½ cups frozen whole kernel corn
1 (14¾ ounces) can cream-style corn
¼ cup cornstarch
1 cup milk
Salt and pepper to taste
1½ cup (6 ounces) cheddar cheese, shredded

Cook bacon, cool and crumble. Using 2 tablespoons bacon drippings; sauté onion, bell pepper and garlic, about 3 minutes. Add fully cooked chicken, chicken broth, frozen corn and cream-style corn. Combine cornstarch with cold milk and stir in soup. Heat to boiling point, reduce heat and simmer 15 minutes. Add salt, pepper and cheese; stir until cheese is melted. Serve.

~°~°~°~°~°~°~°~°~°~°~°~°~°

Hamburger Rice Soup

1 pound lean ground beef or turkey
2 (14.5 ounces) cans tomatoes, diced
2 cups potatoes, cubed
2 carrots, chopped
1 onion, chopped
Salt and pepper to taste
½ teaspoon chili powder
1 teaspoon garlic salt
1 cup frozen corn
¾ cup short white rice, uncooked
5 cups low sodium beef flavoured broth
1 cup water

In a large saucepan over medium heat, cook meat for 5 minutes, or until no longer pink. Drain the excess fat and tomatoes with liquid, potatoes, carrots, onions, salt and pepper, garlic salt, chili powder, rice, corn and water. Bring to boil, stir in broth and reduce heat to low. Simmer (can use crock pot) for at least 1 hour.

~°~°~°~°~°~°~°~°~°~°~°~°~°

Lentil Stew with Sausage

You can easily double or triple the recipe for a larger group or for make ahead leftovers.

1/3 pound of bacon (about 5 thick slices), cut into 1 inch x ¼ inch strips
1 medium-large yellow or white onion, chopped (about 1¼ cups)
2-3 large carrots, diced (2/3 cup)
2-3 large ribs celery, diced (2/3 cup)
1 teaspoon ground cumin
2 cloves garlic, minced (about 2 teaspoons)
1 pound brown or green dry lentils, rinsed and pick over
3 cups water
3 cups chicken stock* (can sub water for a total of 6 cups of liquid)
½ teaspoon dry thyme
1 bay leaf
½ pound Italian sausage (mild, sweet, or spicy, your choice) or smoked sausage, in links (about 2-3 links)
1 teaspoon sherry vinegar (or sub cider vinegar)
¼ cup chopped fresh parsley, with a little extra for garnish
    * If cooking gluten-free, use gluten-free stock.

Heat a large, thick-bottomed pot (6-8 quart) on medium heat. Add the bacon and cook until much of the fat has rendered out and the bacon is browned and cooked through, about 10 minutes. Use a slotted spoon to remove bacon from pan to a dish, set aside. Remove (and reserve for another use) all but 2 tablespoons of bacon fat.

Heat the remaining fat on medium high and add the carrots, onions, celery, and cumin. Stirring frequently, scraping up the browned bits at the bottom of the pan, cook until softened, about 5-7 minutes. Add the garlic and cook a minute more, until fragrant.

Add back in the cooked bacon, the rinsed lentils, stock, water, thyme, bay leaf. At this point add a teaspoon of salt and some pepper. You will season more to taste later. Bring to a boil and reduce the heat to a simmer. Cook partially covered until lentils are tender, about 40 minutes.

While the lentils are cooking, heat a frying pan on medium heat. Add the Italian sausage links. Gently cook, browning on all sides, until just cooked through. Remove from pan, let cool enough to handle. Cut into pieces of desired length (1-2 inches) and add to stew for the last 10 minutes of cooking.

Add sherry vinegar and parsley to stew. Add salt and freshly ground black pepper to taste. You may need to add more salt than you expect, especially if you are making the stew with water only and not water and stock.

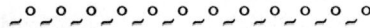

Beef Bouillon Soup

3-4 pounds beef soup bones
Salt and pepper
2 onions, peeled and quartered
2 carrots, cut into 1-inch sections
Zest of one orange, removed in strips with a vegetable peeler
1 cup dry white wine
4 quarts water
1/3 cup fresh cranberries
10 ounces mushrooms, chopped coarse
3 celery, cut into 1 inch sections
4 sprigs of thyme or ½ teaspoon dried thyme
1 bay leaf
4 cloves
1 teaspoon peppercorns

Preheat the oven to 450 °F. In a large roasting pan combine the soup bones and seasoned with salt and pepper, the onions, the carrots, and the zest. Roast mixture in the middle of the oven, turning the bones till browned, and transfer it to a large stockpot.

Deglaze the roasting pan with the wine over high heat, scraping up the brown bits, and add the deglazing liquid to the stockpot or crock pot with the water, cranberries, mushrooms, celery, thyme, bay leaf, cloves, and peppercorns. Bring the liquid to a boil, skimming the froth, and simmer gently, uncovered, for 3 hours.

Ladle the mixture through a sieve lined with a rinsed and squeezed kitchen towel into a large bowl. Discard the remaining solids. The bouillon can be made 3 days in advance and kept chilled. Discard excess fat (leave enough to cover soup when chilled). Bring the bouillon just to a boil and ladle it into warmed bowls.

Makes 8 cups. Serves 6 to 8.

~°~°~°~°~°~°~°~°~°~°~°~°~°~°

Cream of Mushroom Soup

1 pound regular white mushrooms, cleaned, quartered or sliced
1 tablespoon lemon juice
1 tablespoon unsalted butter
2 tablespoons shallots, minced
1 tablespoon chopped fresh thyme or 1 teaspoon dried thyme
½ bay leaf
1 teaspoon salt
½ teaspoon fresh ground pepper
2 cups heavy cream
1½ cups chicken stock
1 teaspoon cornstarch dissolved in 1 tablespoon water
Minced parsley for garnish

In a food processor, coarsely chop mushrooms and lemon juice.

Melt butter in (4-5 quart) sauce pan and lightly sauté shallots on medium heat. Add mushrooms, thyme and bay leaf, sauté over moderate heat for 10-15 minutes, or until the liquid that is released from the mushrooms disappears.

Add salt, pepper, cream and chicken stock and bring to boil. Reduce heat and simmer for 20 minutes.

Add cornstarch and simmer for 10 minutes, stirring constantly. Correct seasoning and add more lemon juice to taste.

Serves 4. Serve sprinkled with a little parsley.

~°~°~°~°~°~°~°~°~°~°~°~°~°

Chickpea and Pasta Soup

1 tablespoon olive oil
7 cloves garlic, minced
2 tablespoons chopped fresh rosemary
2 cups crushed tomatoes
2 cups low fat, low sodium chicken broth
1 cup cooked chickpeas
1 cup cooked elbow macaroni salt and pepper to taste

In a large pot over medium heat, combine the oil and garlic and sauté for 3 minutes. Stir in the rosemary and sauté for 2 more minutes. Add the tomatoes and simmer for 15 minutes.

Add the broth and chickpeas and simmer for an additional 10 minutes. Finally, add the macaroni and allow to heat through completely, about 5 more minutes. Season with salt and pepper to taste and serve.

~°~°~°~°~°~°~°~°~°~°~°~°~°

> *"The greatest pleasure in life is to do what people*
> *say you cannot do."*
> —*Walter Bagehot*

Ham and Brown Bean Soup

1 pound dry pinto beans
8 cups water
1 large, meaty ham hock
1 large onion, chopped
2 cloves garlic, minced
1 teaspoon chili powder
1 teaspoon salt, or to taste
¼ teaspoon ground black pepper, or to taste

Place the beans and water in a large stockpot. Add the ham hock, onion and garlic. Season with chili powder, salt and pepper. Bring to a boil, and cook for 2 minutes. Cover, and remove from heat. Let stand for one hour.

Return the pot to the heat, and bring to a boil once again. Reduce heat to medium-low, and simmer for at least 3 hours to blend flavors. The longer you simmer, the thicker the broth will become or about 6 hours.

Remove the ham hock from the broth, and let cool. Remove the meat from the bone, and return the meat to the stockpot, discarding the bone. Adjust seasonings to taste.

.°.~°.~°.~°.~°.~°.~°.~°.~°.~°.~°.~°

Barley, Lentil and Mushroom Soup

¼ cup olive oil
1 medium onion, chopped
1 stalk celery, chopped
2 carrots, chopped

¾ cup pearl barley
¾ cup dry brown lentils
1/3 cup dried porcini mushrooms, rinsed
2 quarts low-sodium beef broth
1/4 teaspoon dried thyme
1 teaspoon dried parsley
¼ teaspoon freshly ground black pepper
1 bay leaf
4 cups sliced button mushrooms
1 tablespoon dry sherry (optional)

Heat the olive oil in a large pot over medium heat. Add the onion; cook and stir until onions are limp, but not brown, about 5 minutes. Mix in the celery and carrot; cook for another 5 minutes. Stir in the barley and lentils so they are coated with oil, continue to cook and stir until lightly toasted.

Pour in the beef broth and season with thyme, parsley, pepper and the bay leaf. Bring to a boil. Add the porcini mushrooms, cover and simmer for 25 minutes over low heat. Add the button mushroom, cover and continue cooking for another 30 minutes, stirring occasionally. Mix in sherry during the last 5 minutes. Taste and adjust seasoning if needed before serving.

_o_ _o_ _o_ _o_ _o_ _o_ _o_ _o_ _o_ _o_ _o_ _o_ _o_ _o_

White Bean, Spinach, and Barley Stew

1 cup uncooked pearl barley
3 cups water
1 teaspoon olive oil
1 cup chopped yellow onion
2 cloves garlic, minced
½ teaspoon dried rosemary
3/4 cup small fresh mushrooms
1 cup chopped yellow bell pepper

2 tablespoons white wine
1 (15.5 ounces) can white beans, drained and rinsed
1 (14.5 ounces) can Italian-style diced tomatoes, drained
2 cups fresh spinach
1 pinch red pepper flakes

Bring the barley and water to a boil in a pot. Cover, reduce heat to low, and simmer 30 minutes, or until tender.

Heat the olive oil in a large pot over medium heat, and cook the onion and garlic until tender. Season with rosemary. Mix the mushrooms, yellow bell pepper, and wine into the pot, and cook 5 minutes. Stir in the cooked barley, beans, tomatoes, and spinach. Season with red pepper flakes. Continue cooking 10 minutes, or until spinach is wilted.

~°~°~°~°~°~°~°~°~°~°~°~°~°~°

White Bean 'N' Barley Soup

1½ cups dried Great Northern beans
1 large onion, chopped
2 garlic cloves, minced
1 tablespoon olive or canola oil
4 cups vegetable or chicken broth
4 cups water
3 medium carrots, sliced
2 medium red bell peppers, diced
2 celery ribs, chopped
½ cup medium pearl barley
½ cup minced fresh parsley, divided
2 bay leaves
1 teaspoon salt
½ teaspoon dried thyme
½ teaspoon pepper
1 (28 ounces) can diced tomatoes, undrained

Place beans in a Dutch oven or soup kettle; add enough water to cover beans by 2 inches. Bring to a boil; boil for 2 minutes. Remove from the heat; cover and let stand for 1 hour.

Drain and rinse beans, discarding liquid. In a Dutch oven, sauté onion and garlic in oil. Add the broth, water, beans, carrots, red peppers, celery, barley, 1/4 cup parsley, bay leaves, salt, thyme and pepper. Bring to a boil. Reduce heat; cover and simmer for 1 hour or until beans are tender. Add the tomatoes; heat through. Discard bay leaves. Sprinkle with remaining parsley.

_°_°_°_°_°_°_°_°_°_°_°_°_°_°

Winter Lentil Vegetable Soup

½ cup red or green lentils
1 cup chopped onion
1 stalk celery, chopped
2 cups shredded cabbage
1 (28 ounces) can whole peeled tomatoes, chopped
2 cups chicken broth
3 carrots, chopped
1 clove garlic, crushed
1 teaspoon salt
½ teaspoon ground black pepper
¼ teaspoon white sugar
½ teaspoon dried basil
½ teaspoon dried thyme
¼ teaspoon curry powder

Place the lentils into a stockpot or a Dutch oven and add water to twice the depth of the lentils. Bring to a boil, then lower heat and let simmer for about 15 minutes. Drain and rinse lentils; return them to the pot.

149

Add onion, celery, cabbage, tomatoes, chicken broth, carrots and garlic to the pot and season with salt, pepper, sugar, basil, thyme and curry. Cook, simmering for 1½-2 hours or until desired tenderness is achieved.

~°~°~°~°~°~°~°~°~°~°~°~°~°~°~°

"The journey of a thousand miles begins with a single step."—Lao Tzu

Split Pea Soup with Tofu

1 tablespoon olive oil
1 white onion, finely chopped
3 cloves garlic, pressed
4 small red potatoes, diced
1 cup peeled, diced carrots
1 pound dry green split peas
4 cups vegetable broth
1 (16 ounces) package soft tofu
1 (6 ounces) bag fresh spinach, finely chopped
1 tablespoon dried basil salt and pepper to taste

Heat the olive oil in a skillet over medium heat, and sauté the onion and garlic until tender.

In a large pot, mix the onion mixture, potatoes, carrots, and split peas. Pour in the vegetable broth. Bring to a boil, reduce heat to low, and simmer 1 hour.

In food processor, blend the tofu and spinach until creamy, and mix into the pot. Season with basil, salt, and pepper. Cook 1 hour. If the soup becomes too thick, add water. Serve hot.

~°~°~°~°~°~°~°~°~°~°~°~°~°~°~°

Tofu Noodle Soup

2 tablespoons butter
2 cups sliced carrots
1½ cups onions, chopped
1½ cups celery, chopped
1½ teaspoons garlic, minced
12 cups vegetarian chicken-flavoured broth
2 cups egg noodles
1 (14 ounces) container extra-firm tofu, drained and cubed
½ teaspoon dried basil
½ teaspoon dried oregano
¼ teaspoon poultry seasoning
¼ teaspoon dried thyme
¼ teaspoon dried rosemary
¼ teaspoon dried marjoram
¼ teaspoon black pepper
¼ cup cornstarch
3 tablespoons cold water

Melt the butter in a stockpot over medium heat. Stir in the carrots, onions, celery, and garlic and cook until just tender, about 10 minutes.

Pour in the broth and bring to a boil over high heat. Once boiling, add the noodles, tofu, basil, oregano, poultry seasoning, thyme, rosemary, marjoram, and pepper. Dissolve the cornstarch and water in a small bowl. Stir the cornstarch mixture into the soup. Return soup to a boil, then reduce heat to medium-low, cover, and simmer for 30 minutes.

"Hunger is not debatable."—*Harry Hopkins*

Savoury Beef Stew

½ cup all-purpose flour
1 teaspoon salt
2-3 pounds lean beef stew meat, cut into 1-inch cubes
10 small onions or 3 large, diced
2 cups cranberry juice, divided or full bodied dark beer
1 (14.5 ounces) can beef broth
1 cup canned tomatoes, drained
2 cloves garlic, peeled, chopped
1 bay leaf
½ teaspoon pepper
½ teaspoon dried marjoram
¼ teaspoon dried thyme
½ teaspoon rosemary
6 whole juniper berries
5 medium carrots, cut into chunks
5 medium potatoes, peeled and cubed
1 small turnip, cubed
1 small parsnip, cut into ½ inch chunks

Combine flour and salt if desired; coat beef cubes. Reserve remaining flour mixture. Place beef in a Dutch oven. Bake, uncovered, @ 400 °F for 30 minutes. Add onions, garlic, 1-1/2 cups cranberry juice (beer), broth and seasonings. Cover and bake @ 350 °F for 1 hour. Add carrots, turnip, parsnip and potatoes; bake 1 hour or until meat and vegetables are tender. Combine reserved flour mixture and remaining cranberry juice (beer) until smooth; stir into stew. Cover and bake 30 minutes longer. Remove bay leaf. Return to the oven for 5 minutes.

Note: this recipe can be done in a slow cooker. Cook meat, onions, garlic, broth, seasonings and preferred juice for 3-3½ hours before adding vegetables.

MY SPECIAL RECIPES

Chapter Five

Cakes

"It's the company, not the cooking, that makes a meal."
Kirby Larson

Hint:
How to Make Vanilla Extract:
Commercial vanilla extract usually has simple syrup (sugar water) added to the extract to give it a sweet aftertaste. You can do this if you want, but if you are using the vanilla for baking, there really is no need.

3 vanilla beans
1 cup vodka
glass jar with tight fitting lid

Use kitchen scissors or a sharp paring knife to cut lengthwise down each vanilla bean, splitting them in half, leaving an inch at the end connected.
Put vanilla beans in u glass jar or bottle with a tight fitting lid (mason jars work well). Cover completely with the vodka.

Give the bottle a good shake every once in a while. Store in a dark, cool place for 2 months or longer.

Lasts for years. You can keep topping it off with vodka once in a while as you use it, just remember to give it a good shake.

You can also make vanilla sugar by putting a split vanilla bean into a jar of white, granulated sugar. Great way to infuse the sugar with vanilla flavour for baking.

~°~°~°~°~°~°~°~°~°~°~°~°~°

Pineapple Upside Down Cake

3 tablespoons butter
1 (20 ounces) can crushed pineapple with juice
8 maraschino cherries
¼ cup walnut halves
2/3 cup packed brown sugar
1/3 cup shortening
½ cup white sugar
1 egg
1 teaspoon vanilla extract
1¼ cups sifted cake flour
1½ teaspoons baking powder
½ teaspoon salt
½ cup reserved pineapple juice

Preheat oven to 350 °F (175 °C). Drain pineapple and reserve ½ cup of the juice.

Melt butter in a 9 inches round pan. Arrange cherries and walnut halves in the pan according to how many servings you want. Sprinkle with brown sugar, and then pineapple.

Cream together shortening and granulated sugar until light and fluffy. Add egg and vanilla, and beat well. Sift together flour, baking powder and salt. Add alternately with reserved pineapple syrup, beating after each addition.

Spread batter in pan over pineapple. Bake at 350 °F (175 °C) for 45-50 minutes. Let stand 5 minutes in the pan, then invert onto plate. Serve warm.

~°~°~°~°~°~°~°~°~°~°~°~°~°

TIP:
<u>Need</u> *extra ice cubes . . . Freeze water in clean plastic egg cartons, then transfer the ice to sandwich bags and store it in the freezer.*

Persimmon Upside Down Cake

For the Topping:
3 tablespoons margarine
¼ cup brown sugar
4 large ripe persimmons, peeled and sliced

For the Cake:
½ cup butter, softened
1 cup white sugar
2 cups persimmon pulp
2 cups sifted all-purpose flour
2 teaspoons baking powder
1 teaspoon baking soda
¼ teaspoon salt
½ teaspoon ground cinnamon
½ teaspoon ground nutmeg
½ teaspoon ground cloves
½ cup chopped pecans
½ teaspoon lemon zest

Preheat an oven to 350 °F (175 °C). Grease a 9 inches round cake pan.

Place the margarine and brown sugar in the cake pan and transfer the pan to the hot oven until the sugar is melted and bubbly, about 5 minutes. Remove from the oven; arrange the persimmon slices over the topping in the cake pan.

Beat the butter and sugar with an electric mixer in a large bowl until light and fluffy. The mixture should be noticeably lighter in color. Stir in the persimmon pulp. In a separate bowl, combine the flour, baking powder, baking soda, salt, cinnamon, nutmeg, and cloves. Gradually add the flour mixture to the batter, stirring just to mix. The batter will be stiff, since the only liquid comes from the persimmon pulp. Stir in the pecans and lemon zest.

Spoon the cake batter evenly over the persimmon slices and return the cake pan to the preheated oven. Bake until a toothpick inserted into the center comes out clean, about 30 minutes. Cool in the pan for 10 minutes before inverting the cake right-side-up on a serving platter.

~°~°~°~°~°~°~°~°~°~°~°~°~°

Plum Blueberry Upside Down Cake

1¼ cups all-purpose flour
1½ teaspoons baking powder
¼ teaspoon salt
3 tablespoons margarine
¼ cup brown sugar
1/3 cup margarine
1 cup white sugar
1 egg
1 teaspoon vanilla
¾ cup milk
4 black plums, pitted and thinly sliced
¾ cup blueberries

Preheat oven to 350 °F (175 °C). Grease a 9 inch cake pan. Combine the flour, baking powder and salt. Set aside.

In the prepared pan, combine 3 tablespoons margarine and brown sugar. Place pan inside the preheated oven until the margarine melts and begins to bubble. Set aside. In a large bowl, cream together the 1/3 cup margarine and 1 cup white sugar until light and fluffy. Beat in the egg, stir in the vanilla. Beat in the flour mixture alternately with the milk, mixing just until incorporated.

Arrange plums around the edges of the prepared pan, overlapping slightly. Distribute the blueberries in the center. Pour batter into prepared pan, covering fruit completely. Bake in the preheated oven for 40 minutes, or until a toothpick inserted into the center of the cake comes out clean. Allow to cool 15 minutes before serving.

Floating Brownie

¾ cup white sugar
2 tablespoons butter
½ cup milk
1 teaspoon vanilla
1 cup all-purpose flour
¼ teaspoon salt
1 teaspoon baking powder
3 tablespoons unsweetened cocoa powder
½ cup white sugar
½ cup packed brown sugar
¼ cup unsweetened cocoa powder
1¼ cups strong brewed coffee, boiling

Cream together ¾ cup sugar and butter. Add the milk and vanilla and mix. Sift together the flour, salt, baking powder, and 3 tablespoons cocoa, and add to the mixture.

Spread into a greased 9 x 9 inch pan. The batter will be thick.

Combine ½ cup white sugar, ½ cup brown sugar, and ¼ cup cocoa. Sprinkle this over the batter.

Finally, pour 1¼ cups boiling double strength coffee or water evenly over all. Bake at 350 °F (175 °C) to 375 °F (190 °C) for 30 minutes. Serves 6 to 8.

~°~°~°~°~°~°~°~°~°~°~°~°~°

Fudge Ribbon Cake

1 (8 ounce) package cream cheese
¼ cup white sugar
1 egg
½ teaspoon vanilla
1 cup all-purpose flour
1 1/3 cups white sugar
1¼ teaspoons baking powder
½ teaspoon salt
¼ teaspoon baking soda
1 cup milk
3 tablespoons shortening
1 egg
½ teaspoon vanilla
3 (1 ounce) squares unsweetened chocolate, melted
3 (1 ounce) squares semisweet chocolate
1 tablespoon butter
1 tablespoon water
½ teaspoon vegetable oil

In a small bowl, beat together cream cheese, ¼ cup sugar, 1 egg, and ½ teaspoon vanilla until smooth.

In a separate bowl, combine flour, 1 1/3 cup sugar, baking powder, soda, salt, milk, shortening, 1 egg, ½ teaspoon vanilla, and 3 squares melted unsweetened chocolate in large mixing bowl. Beat for ½ minute with an electric mixer on low speed. Beat 2 minutes on medium speed.

Grease a 9 inch square pan. Pour half of the batter into the pan. Spread cream cheese mixture evenly over the batter, and top with remaining cake batter to cover completely.

Bake at 350 °F (175 °C) for 50 to 55 minutes, or until cake tester inserted in center comes out clean. Cool.

Melt 3 squares semisweet chocolate with butter, water, and oil; blend until smooth. Spread evenly over cooled cake.

_°_°_°_°_°_°_°_°_°_°_°_°_°_°_°

Apple Sauce Raisin Molasses Cake

1/3 cup butter
½ cup sugar
2 eggs, well beaten
½ cup molasses
2 cups flour
3 teaspoons baking powder
1 teaspoon cinnamon
½ teaspoon nutmeg
¼ teaspoon cloves
1/8 teaspoon baking soda
1 cup apple sauce
½ cup raisins

Cream butter, add sugar slowly beating well, add eggs, beat well, add molasses.

Sift dry ingredients; add alternating with apple sauce into butter mixture. Add raisins.

Bake in 8 inch square pan @ 350 °F for 1 hour.

_°_°_°_°_°_°_°_°_°_°_°_°_°_°_°

TIP:
Much of the heavy cake and bread is the result of the oven door being slammed. Close as gently as possible.

~°~°~°~°~°~°~°~°~°~°~°~°~°

Amazing Raisin Cake

Beat together at low speed for 2 minutes:
3 cups flour
1 cup mayonnaise
2 eggs
1½ teaspoons cinnamon
½ teaspoon salt
2 cups sugar
1/3 cup milk
2 teaspoons baking soda
½ teaspoon nutmeg
¼ teaspoon cloves

Stir in apples, raisins and nuts spoon into greased 13 x 9 inch pan.

Bake @ 350 °F for 45 minutes. Frost with whipping cream.

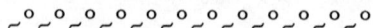

Harvest Spice Cake

1 cup butter
3 eggs
1 cup apple, chopped
1 cup sour cream
1¼ cups sugar
2½ cups flour

¼ teaspoon cloves and allspice
1 tablespoon orange peel
1 teaspoon baking powder
1 teaspoon baking soda
1 teaspoon salt
1 teaspoon cinnamon
1 cup raisins and nuts

Cream butter, sugar and orange peel. Beat in eggs one at a time. Combine dry ingredients, combine sour cream and apples. Add alternately with sour cream mixture, stir in nuts and raisins

Bake in 10 inch tube pan, greased. Bake @ 350 °F for 55-60 minutes.

Prune Layer Cake

½ cup butter
1 cup granulated sugar
3 eggs
2 ¼ cups all purpose flour
1 teaspoon baking soda
1 teaspoon baking powder
1/8 teaspoon salt
1 teaspoon cinnamon
1 teaspoon nutmeg
1 teaspoon allspice
1 cup prune juice
1 cup prunes, cooked, chopped

Cream butter, add sugar gradually; beat until light and fluffy. Add unbeaten eggs, one at a time, beating well after each addition. Sift together flour, baking powder, baking soda, salt and spices. Add sifted ingredients alternately with prune juice to creamed mixture. Beat until blended. Fold in chopped prunes. Pour into 2 greased 9 inch layer pans.

Bake @ 350 °F for 30-40 minutes. Cool.

Ice with a vanilla, butterscotch or maple icing.

> *"Preach not to others what they should eat, but eat as becomes you, and be silent. "—Epictetus*

ᵒ ᵒ ᵒ ᵒ ᵒ ᵒ ᵒ ᵒ ᵒ ᵒ ᵒ ᵒ ᵒ ᵒ

Rhubarb Orange Coffee Cake

Topping: ¼ cup brown sugar
1 tablespoon orange peel
½ teaspoon cinnamon
Cake: 2 cups flour
¾ cup sugar
2 teaspoon baking powder
½ teaspoon baking soda
½ teaspoon salt
1 egg
1 teaspoon vanilla
1/3 cup orange juice
1½ cup rhubarb, chopped

Combine dry ingredients; combine wet ingredients; blend together. Spread ½ batter into pan, cover with rhubarb and add remaining batter to cover.

Bake @ 350 °F for 45 minutes in a 8 inches square pan.

ᵒ ᵒ ᵒ ᵒ ᵒ ᵒ ᵒ ᵒ ᵒ ᵒ ᵒ ᵒ ᵒ ᵒ

Apple Cake

1 cup all purpose flour
1 teaspoon salt
1 teaspoon ground cinnamon
1 teaspoon ground nutmeg
½ teaspoon baking soda
½ cup butter, softened
1 cup granulated sugar
1 egg
2 cups apples, peeled, chopped
1 cup nuts chopped
¼ cup butter
¼ cup sugar
¼ cup brown sugar
¼ cup whipping cream
½ teaspoon vanilla
Whipping cream (optional)

Grease an 8 x 8 x 2 inches baking pan; set aside. Stir together the flour, salt, cinnamon, nutmeg and baking soda; set aside.

In a large mixing bowl, beat the ½ cup butter, add 1 cup granulated sugar; beat until combined. Beat in egg, then flour mixture just until combined. Stir in apples and nuts. Spread in prepared pan. Bake @ 350 °F for 40 minutes or until a toothpick inserted near the center comes out clean.

In a small saucepan, melt the butter, sugar, brown sugar, and whipping cream, stirring constantly. Stir in vanilla. Pour mixture over hot cake. If desired serve with whipped cream

_°_°_°_°_°_°_°_°_°_°_°_°_°_°_°

Apple and Fig Cake

1¼ cups vegetable oil
2 cups brown sugar
3 large eggs
3 tablespoons dark rum
2 cups all-purpose flour
1 cup whole wheat flour
1½ teaspoons cinnamon
1 teaspoon salt
1 teaspoon baking soda
¼ teaspoon allspice, ground
¼ teaspoon ginger, ground
1/8 teaspoon cloves, ground
3 cups apples, peeled, diced small
1 cup walnuts, roasted, coarsely chopped
½ cup dried figs, chopped
Caramel Rum Sauce: 1 cup white sugar
3 tablespoons cold water
1 cup whipping cream
2 tablespoons butter
3 tablespoons dark rum
2 teaspoons vanilla

Preheat the oven to 350 °F. Lightly oil a 10-12 cup Bundt pan. Blend the vegetable oil and brown sugar until smooth; add the eggs one at a time until combined. Stir in the rum and set aside.

In a separate bowl, combine the two flours, cinnamon, salt, baking soda, allspice, ginger and cloves. Add to the egg mixture and continue to mix until thoroughly combined. Stir in apples, walnuts and figs until evenly distributed throughout the batter.

Pour into bundt pan and bake for 60 minutes. Cool for 15 minutes. Using a sharp knife run around the sides of the pan to loosen the cake, invert and cool completely. Serve with the caramel rum sauce.

To make the caramel sauce: Place the sugar and water in a small, heavy-bottomed pan over medium heat. As the sugar begins to melt, swirl the pan around gently over the heat. When the sugar has completely melted, increase the heat to medium-high and let the mixture boil. Once the mixture turns to a light amber, swirl the pan again to distribute the sugar evenly. As the sugar turns from amber to a dark golden, remove from the heat and slowly add the whipping cream. Be careful as the cream may bubble over. Reduce the heat to medium-low and return mixture to the heat. Stir until mixture is completely smooth. The sugar may turn into a hard ball, but will eventually melt into the cream. Remove from the heat and stir in the butter, vanilla and rum. Store refrigerated until ready to use. Reheat before serving.

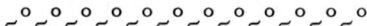

Molasses Cake

2 ¼ cups flour
1 cup sugar
¼ teaspoon salt
½ cup melted butter
½ cup dark molasses
1 teaspoon baking soda
½ cup boiling water

Combine molasses, baking soda and boiling water in large bowl . . . it foams up. In separate bowl combine remaining ingredients. Mixture will be crumbly, save approx 2 tablespoons of crumbly mixture for topping. Mix molasses mixture with crumbly mixture, just until incorporated. Pour batter into round shallow cake pan, sprinkle with remaining crumbly mixture as topping. Bake 350 °F for approx 45 minutes.

<u>MY SPECIAL RECIPES</u>

Chapter Six

Desserts and Pies

"The discovery of a new dish does more
for human happiness than the
discovery of a new star."
—Jean Anthelme Brillat-Savarin

Hint:
How to Make a Lattice Top for a Pie Crust
Before starting the lattice top, roll out half of your pie dough and line your pie dish with it. The dough should extend beyond the rim of the pie dish by about half an inch. Put it in the refrigerator to chill while you work on the lattice. On a lightly floured surface, roll out the other half of your pie dough to the same extent as the first half (about 3 inches beyond the diameter of your pie dish). It's easier to work with the dough if it is chilled, so if it the dough has softened too much, put the rolled-out piece on a flat cookie sheet and chill it in the refrigerator or freezer for a few minutes.

Cut the dough into even strips, ½ inch-¾ inch wide, depending on how thick you want your lattice strips. You can use a blunt knife with or without a ruler or straight edge to guide you, or you can use a pizza wheel or a pastry wheel if you have one.

Fill your pie shell with the pie filling. Lay out 4-7 parallel strips of the pie dough, depending on how thick your strips are, on top of the filling, with about ½ inch-¾ inch space between them. Fold back every other strip.

Place one long strip of dough perpendicular to the parallel strips as shown. Unfold the folded strips over the perpendicular strip.

Now take the parallel strips that are running underneath the perpendicular strip and fold them back over the perpendicular strip, as shown. Lay down a second perpendicular strip of dough next to the first strip, with some space between the strips. Unfold the folded parallel strips over the second strip.

Continue this process until the weave is complete over the top of the pie.

Trim the edges of the strips flush with the dough of the underlying pie dish, which should be about half an inch over the sides. Fold back the rim of the shell over the edge of the lattice strips, and crimp to secure.

TIP:
Baking Apples
Prick the skin of the apples and they will cook without bursting.

Try using milk instead of water when making pie crusts to make a more tender crust and to have it brown nicely.

Lemon Puff Pie

1 pouch (113g) Lemon Pie filling
1/3 cup sugar
2¼ cups water
2 eggs, separated
1 (9 inches) pie crust, baked and cooled
¼ cup sugar

Combine pie filling mix, 1/3 cup sugar and ¼ cup of the water in saucepan; blend in egg yolks. Add remaining 2 cups water. Cook and stir over medium heat until mixture comes to a full boil and thickens. Remove from heat. Pour half the filling into pie shell.

Beat egg whites until foamy. Add remaining sugar gradually, beating after each addition. Continue beating until mixture forms stiff peaks.

Gently fold in remaining hot filling into meringue. Let stand 10 minutes. Spread evenly over pie filling in shell. Chill until set.

TIP:

Make an ice cream sandwich by putting a scoop between two large biscuits or splitting a trifle sponge in half and filling it.

Hollow out a fairy cake to make a little edible bowl.

⌐°⌐°⌐°⌐°⌐°⌐°⌐°⌐°⌐°⌐°⌐°⌐°⌐°

Sour Cream Citrus Fluff

1 cup chocolate graham crumbs
2 tablespoons margarine, melted
1 teaspoon lemon rind, grated
1 teaspoon lime rind, grated
25 large white marshmallows
¼ cup sugar
¼ cup water
2 tablespoons lemon juice
2 tablespoons lime juice
½ cup sour cream
1 drop green food colouring
1 envelope dessert topping mix

Combine crumbs, margarine, lemon and lime rind. Press 2/3 mixture evenly over bottom of 8 inch square pan. Reserve remaining crumb mixture for topping. Combine marshmallows, sugar, water, lemon and lime juices in medium saucepan. Stir over medium heat until marshmallows melt. Cool to room temperature. Stir in sour cream and food colouring. Prepare topping mix as per package. Fold in citrus mixture. Pour into prepared pan and sprinkle remaining crumb mixture over top. Chill until set.

~°~°~°~°~°~°~°~°~°~°~°~°~°~°

Homemade Mince Pie with Crumbly Topping

½ cup cold butter
1½ cups all-purpose flour
½ teaspoon salt
½ cup cold water
1½ cups raisins
5 apples, peeled, cored and chopped
2 tablespoons finely chopped grapefruit peel without white layer
1/3 cup orange juice
½ cup apple cider
¾ cup white sugar
½ teaspoon ground cinnamon
¼ teaspoon ground cloves
½ graham cracker, crushed
1/3 cup white sugar
¾ cup all-purpose flour
6 tablespoons butter
½ graham cracker, crushed

Preheat oven to 425 °F (220 °C).

In a bowl, mix together ½ cup of cold butter with 1½ cups flour and the salt with a fork until the mixture is very crumbly. Mix in water, a tablespoon at a time, just until the mixture holds together. Mix again with a fork, turn out onto a floured pastry cloth. Pat the dough out into a round piece, and roll out into a 10-inch circle. Invert a 9-inch pie dish onto the dough. Flip the dough over, and peel from the pastry cloth; adjust the crust into the plate if necessary. Fold the dough over the edge of the pie dish. Set the crust aside.

Combine the raisins, apples, grapefruit peel, orange juice, and apple cider in a saucepan, and bring to a simmer over medium heat. Cook, stirring occasionally, until the apple pieces are soft, about 15 minutes. Stir in ¾ cup of sugar, the cinnamon, cloves, and half a crushed graham cracker, and mix well.

Mix together 1/3 cup of sugar, ¾ cup of flour, 6 tablespoons of butter, and half a crushed graham cracker in a bowl, stirring until the mixture looks like fine crumbs. Pour the mince filling into the prepared pie crust, and sprinkle evenly with the streusel topping.

Bake in the preheated oven for 15 minutes, and reduce oven temperature to 350 °F (175 °C); bake until the topping is lightly browned, about 30 more minutes. Allow to cool before serving.

$_\sim^{\circ}{}_\sim^{\circ}{}_\sim^{\circ}{}_\sim^{\circ}{}_\sim^{\circ}{}_\sim^{\circ}{}_\sim^{\circ}{}_\sim^{\circ}{}_\sim^{\circ}{}_\sim^{\circ}{}_\sim^{\circ}{}_\sim^{\circ}$

Dutch Apple Pie with Oatmeal Streusel

1 (9 inch) pie shell
5 cups apples, peeled, cored and sliced
2 tablespoons all-purpose flour
2/3 cup white sugar
½ teaspoon ground cinnamon
¼ teaspoon ground nutmeg
¼ teaspoon ground allspice
2 tablespoons butter
¾ cup all-purpose flour
½ teaspoon ground cinnamon
½ cup brown sugar, packed
¾ cup rolled oats

1 teaspoon lemon zest
½ cup butter

Preheat oven to 425 °F (220 °C). Fit pastry shell into pie pan and place in freezer.

To Make Apple Filling: Place apples in a large bowl. In a separate bowl combine 2 tablespoons flour, white sugar, ½ teaspoon cinnamon, nutmeg, and allspice. Mix well, add to apples. Toss until apples are evenly coated.

Remove pie shell from freezer. Place apple mixture in pie shell and dot with 2 tablespoons butter or margarine. Lay a sheet of aluminum foil lightly on top of filling, but do not seal.

Bake in preheated oven for 10 minutes.

While filling is baking, make Streusel Topping: In a medium bowl combine 3/4 cup flour, ½ teaspoon cinnamon, brown sugar, oats, and lemon peel. Mix thoroughly, cut in ½ cup butter or margarine until mixture is crumbly. Remove filling from oven and sprinkle streusel on top.

Reduce heat to 375 °F (190 °C). Bake an additional 30-35 minutes, until streusel is browned and apples are tender. Cover loosely with aluminum foil to prevent excess browning.

TIP:
Add one-quarter teaspoon soda to cranberries while cooking and they will not require much sugar.

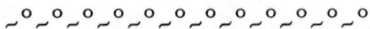

Rhubarb Cobbler

¾ cup white sugar
2 tablespoons cornstarch
4 cups rhubarb, chopped
1 tablespoon water
1 tablespoon butter, diced

1 teaspoon ground cinnamon
1 cup all-purpose flour
1 tablespoon white sugar
1 ½ teaspoons baking powder
¼ teaspoon salt
¼ cup butter
¼ cup milk
1 egg, beaten
2 tablespoons white sugar

Preheat oven to 400 °F (200 °C). Lightly grease a 9 inch square baking dish.

In a saucepan, mix ¾ cup sugar and cornstarch. Stir in the rhubarb and water. Bring to a boil. Cook and stir for 1 minute. Transfer to the prepared baking dish. Dot with butter, and sprinkle with cinnamon.

In a medium bowl, sift together flour, 1 tablespoon sugar, baking powder, and salt. Cut in the butter until the mixture resembles coarse crumbs.

In a small bowl, mix the milk and egg. Add all at once to dry ingredients, stirring just to moisten. Drop by teaspoonfuls on top of the rhubarb mixture. Sprinkle with sugar.

Bake for 20 minutes in the preheated oven, until crisp and lightly browned.

Rhubarb Cobbler with Oat Dumplings

¾ cup sugar
2 tablespoons cornstarch
1 cup water
½ cup orange juice
4 cups sliced fresh or frozen rhubarb
Dumplings:

½ cup all-purpose flour
¼ cup whole wheat flour
¼ cup quick-cooking oats
1 ½ teaspoons baking powder
¼ teaspoon salt
½ cup milk
2 tablespoons vegetable oil
Topping:
1 tablespoon sugar
¼ teaspoon ground cinnamon

In a saucepan, combine sugar and cornstarch. Gradually stir in water and orange juice. Cook and stir until thickened and clear. Add rhubarb and bring to a boil. Remove from the heat. Pour into a 2 quart baking dish. For dumplings, combine flours, oats, baking powder and salt in a bowl. Combine milk and oil; add to flour mixture, stirring lightly until blended. Spoon over rhubarb. Combine topping ingredients; sprinkle over dumplings. Bake at 425 °F for 40 minutes.

~°~°~°~°~°~°~°~°~°~°~°~°~°~°

"Why should we live with such hurry and waste
of life? We are determined to be starved before we
are hungry."—Henry David Thoreau

TIP:

When a custard pie shrinks from the crust, it has been baked in too hot an oven. The oven should be hot for the first eight or ten minutes, in order to bake the pastry so that it will not become soaked with liquid. Then reduce the heat or the custard will boil.

Almond Joy Tart

Almond tart dough:
1 large egg
¼ cup whole almonds, toasted
¼ cup sugar
1 ¼ + 2 tablespoons all-purpose flour
¼ teaspoon salt
½ cup unsalted butter, cold, ½ inch cubes
Coconut cream filling:
8 ounces white chocolate, coarsely chopped
1 cup whipping cream
2 cups shredded coconut, unsweetened
1 tablespoon light rum
Chocolate glaze and garnish:
2 ounces milk chocolate, coarsely chopped
2 ounces dark chocolate, coarsely chopped
½ cup whipping cream
6 whole toasted almonds

Dough and Ganache:

In a small bowl, lightly whisk the egg and set it aside. Put the almonds and sugar in a food processor and pulse until the almonds are finely ground. Add flour and salt and pulse again until mixed. Add the butter and pulse until sandy. Add egg and pulse until the dough begins to form a ball. Form the dough into a disk, wrap it tightly in plastic, refrigerate for at least an hour.

To prepare the white chocolate ganache for filling, place the chocolate in a medium heatproof bowl. In a small saucepan set over medium heat and heat the cream just to a boil. Pour over the chocolate and let stand for 30 seconds. Slowly whisk mixture until smooth. Cover and refrigerate for at least 4 hours.

Bake the tart:

Dust a work surface with flour. Place the dough on surface and divide into six equal parts. Shape each portion into a smooth disk roll to a 5 ½ inch circle 1/8 inch thick. Very gently press into a 4 inch tart pan and freeze for 30 minutes. Preheat oven to 375 °F. Line the tart crusts with aluminum foil and fill each one ¾ full of pie weights or dried beans. Bake for 15 minutes, remove weights and foil and bake another 10 minutes or until lightly brown. Cool.

The Filling and Glaze:

Beat the chilled white chocolate at medium speed until soft peaks form. Do not over whip. Fold in coconut and rum. Divide the filling evenly between the cooled tart shells, chill.

Place the milk and dark chocolates in a medium heatproof bowl. In a small saucepan heat the whipping cream until it is just about to boil. Pour over chocolates, whisk to combine. Let mixture set for 10 minutes. Remove the tarts from the refrigerator and spoon glaze evenly over each one. Top each tart with one almond, refrigerate until the glaze sets about 10 minutes.

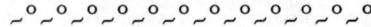

<u>MY SPECIAL RECIPES</u>

Chapter Seven

Cookies

"Our lives are not in the lap of the gods,
but in the lap of our cooks."
—Lin Yutang

<u>*TIP:*</u>
Use pastry wheel to cut rolled cookie dough in squares or diamonds, much less rolling and very pretty.

Rinse measuring cup in hot water before using syrup, oil, etc. Will pour out clean and not stick to cup.

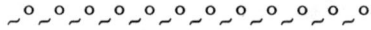

<u>Pumpkin Biscotti</u>

2½ cups flour
1 cup sugar
1 teaspoon baking powder
1 teaspoon cinnamon
½ teaspoon nutmeg
Pinch ginger

Pinch cloves
Pinch salt
2 eggs
½ cup pumpkin purée
1 teaspoon vanilla extract

Preheat oven to 350°F. Sift together the flour, salt, sugar, baking powder, and spices into a large bowl.

In another bowl, whisk together the eggs, pumpkin purée, and vanilla extract. Pour the pumpkin mixture into the flour mixture. Give it a rough stir to generally incorporate the ingredients, the dough will be crumbly.

Flour your hands and a clean kitchen surface and lightly knead the dough. Lightly grease a baking sheet or line it with parchment paper. Form the dough into a large log, roughly about 15-20 inches by 6-7 inches. The loaves should be relatively flat, only about ½ inch high. Bake for 22-30 minutes, until the center is firm to the touch. (Feel free to also form two smaller logs for cute two-bite biscotti; just cut the baking time to 18-24 minutes.)

Let biscotti cool for 15 minutes and then using a serrated knife cut into 1 inch wide pieces. Turn the oven to 300°F and bake for an additional 15-20 minutes. Cool completely.

Biscotti may be still a tad moist and chewy, so if you prefer it crisp let it sit uncovered overnight in a dry space. Serve and enjoy.

Makes approximately 15 cookies.

"Nothing endures but change."—Heraclitus

~°~°~°~°~°~°~°~°~°~°~°~°~°~°~°

Double Ginger Crackle Cookie

2 cups flour
2 teaspoons baking soda
2 teaspoons ginger
½ teaspoon cinnamon
½ teaspoon salt
¼ cup crystallized ginger, finely chopped
¾ cup vegetable shortening
½ cup brown sugar, firmly packed
½ cup sugar
2 tablespoons molasses
1 egg
1 teaspoon lemon peel

Preheat oven to 350 °F. Line cookie sheets with parchment paper.

Beat shortening, brown sugar and sugar until light. Beat in molasses, egg and lemon peel till smooth.

Gradually add in dry ingredients; mixing until smooth.

Form dough into small balls, dip in sugar and place on cookie sheet 2 inches apart.

Bake 10 minutes or until golden brown and crackled on top.

Makes about 4 dozen.

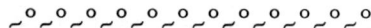

Sugar Cookies

1½ cups sugar
2/3 cup shortening or butter*
2 eggs
2 tablespoons milk
1 teaspoon vanilla

3¼ cups flour
2½ teaspoons baking powder
½ teaspoon salt

Early in the day or the day before: In a large bowl cream the shortening and the sugar. Add the eggs, extract, and milk. In a medium bowl mix the dry ingredients with a wire whisk. Add the dry ingredients to the large bowl. Mix with mixer until well combined. With hands, shape dough into a ball. Wrap with plastic wrap and refrigerate for 2-3 hours.

Preheat oven to 400 °F. Lightly grease cookie sheets. Roll ½ or 1/3 dough at a time, keep the rest refrigerated. For crisp cookies, roll dough, paper thin. For softer cookies, roll 1/8 to ¼ inch thick.

With floured cookie cutter, cut into shapes. Re-roll trimmings and cut. Place cookies ½ inch apart on cookie sheets. Decorate. Bake 8 minutes or until very light brown. With pancake turner, remove cookies to racks; cool. Makes about 6 dozen cookies.

~°~°~°~°~°~°~°~°~°~°~°~°~°~°

Thumbprint Cookies

1 cup butter or margarine, softened
¾ cup sugar
2 large eggs, whites and yolks separated, reserved
1 teaspoon vanilla
2 cups flour
¼ teaspoon salt
1¼ cups finely chopped nuts
½ cup jams, preserves or curds

Beat butter until creamy. Gradually add sugar. Add egg yolks (reserving egg whites) and extract. Mix out 1 cup of flour and add salt to it. Gradually add to butter mixture. Add other cup of flour gradually. Cover and chill at least 1 hour or overnight. Also make sure reserved egg whites are covered and refrigerated, too.

Preheat oven to 350 °F. Very lightly grease 2 cookie sheets. Set counter for the rolling process by setting out low-sided bowl with lightly beaten and reserved egg whites and another low-sided bowl for the nuts. Roll dough into 1 to 1½ inch balls. Then roll each ball into egg white and then nuts. Place on cookie sheets 2 inches apart. Press thumb into each cookie before baking. Bake for 15 minutes. Cool 1 minute on cookie sheet. Move to wire racks for cooling. Press centers again with thumb. When cookies are almost cool, fill centers with jam.

~°~°~°~°~°~°~°~°~°~°~°~°~°

Polish Kolaczki

1 (8 ounces) cream cheese, softened
12 ounces (3 sticks) butter, softened
3 cups all-purpose flour
2 (14-ounces) cans fillings of choice (apricot, prune, raspberry, etc.)
Confectioners' sugar

Mix cream cheese and butter until light and fluffy. Add flour 1 cup at a time and mix well. Wrap dough in plastic and refrigerate for at least 1 hour.

Heat oven to 350 °F. Roll out dough ¼ inch on a surface that has been dusted with equal parts confectioners' and granulated sugars (not flour), because the granulated sugar will act as ball bearings and help keep the dough from sticking. Cut into 2 inches squares. Place ½-1 teaspoon filling on center of each square. Overlap opposite corners of dough to the center over filling.

Bake for 15 minutes or when corners start to brown. Cool and dust with confectioners' sugar. These tend to become soggy if held for several days, so store them tightly covered (or freeze) without the confectioners' sugar. Dust with confectioners' sugar just prior to service.

⁓°⁓°⁓°⁓°⁓°⁓°⁓°⁓°⁓°⁓°⁓°⁓°⁓°

Coconut Kisses—Besitos de Coco

3 cups coconut flakes
½ cup flour
4 egg yolks
1 cup brown sugar
¼ tablespoon butter
2 tablespoons coconut (or vanilla) extract

Preheat oven to 350 °F.

Grease a 13 x 9 x 2 inches cookie sheet.

In a bowl, thoroughly mix all ingredients together into a dough.

Divide the dough into 24 uniform balls.

Place the balls on the greased cookie sheet and bake for about 35 minutes. They should be golden.

⁓°⁓°⁓°⁓°⁓°⁓°⁓°⁓°⁓°⁓°⁓°⁓°⁓°

Melomakarona—Honey Cookies with Walnuts

For the cookies:
1 cup olive oil
1 cup vegetable oil
¾ cup sugar
Zest of one orange
¾ cup orange juice
¼ cup brandy
2 teaspoons baking powder

1 teaspoon baking soda
Pinch of salt
7 ½ cups all purpose flour
¾ cup walnuts, ground coarsely
Ground cinnamon for sprinkling
For the syrup:
1 cup honey
1 cup sugar
1½ cups water
1 cinnamon stick
3-4 whole cloves
1-2 inch piece lemon rind
1 teaspoon lemon juice

Preheat the oven to 350 °F.

In a small bowl, using your fingers, combine the orange zest with the sugar—rubbing the grains as if you were playing with sand to release the orange oils into the sugar.

Using an electric mixer, beat the oil with the orange sugar until well mixed. In a separate bowl, sift the flour with the baking powder, baking soda and salt.

Add the orange juice and brandy to mixer and mix well.

Slowly incorporate the flour cup by cup until the mixture forms a dough that is not too loose but not quite firm either. It will be dense and wet but not sticky. Once the flour is incorporated fully stop mixing.

To roll cookies, pinch a portion of dough off about the size of a walnut. Shape in your palms into a smooth oblong shape, almost like a small egg. Place on an ungreased cookie sheet. Shape and roll cookies until the sheet is filled.

Press the tines of a large fork in a crosshatch pattern in the center of each cookie. This will flatten them slightly in the center. The cookies should resemble lightly flattened ovals when they go in the oven.

Bake in a preheated 350 °F oven for 25-30 minutes until lightly browned. (The cookies will darken when submerged in syrup.)

While the cookies are baking, prepare the syrup.

In a saucepan, combine the honey, sugar, water, cinnamon, cloves, and lemon rind. Bring the mixture to a boil then lower the heat and simmer uncovered for about 10-15 minutes. Remove the cinnamon, cloves, and lemon rind and stir in lemon juice.

Place the ground walnuts in a shallow plate or bowl next to the stove top. When the cookies come out of the oven and while they are still very warm, carefully float the cookies in the syrup and allow the cookies to absorb syrup on both sides.

Using a fork or small spatula, remove the cookie from the syrup and place on a platter or plate. Press ground walnuts lightly into the tops of the cookies (syrup will help it adhere) and sprinkle lightly with ground cinnamon.

Do not refrigerate Melomakarona as they will harden. Store in an airtight container at room temperature.

> *"It's not that some people have willpower and some don't. It's that some people are ready to change and others are not."—James Gordon*

~°~°~°~°~°~°~°~°~°~°~°~°~°~°

Mantecados—Spanish Crumble Cakes

2 ¼ cup vegetable shortening
1 cup vegetable oil
1 2/3 cup granulated sugar
4 egg yolks
2 shot glasses of anise (see note below for substitute)
1 lemon peel, grated juice from 1 lemon
½ teaspoon cinnamon
7 ¼ cups unbleached white flour

½ teaspoon baking soda
1 egg white, beaten for glaze

Substitution Note: Anise-flavoured liqueur can be purchased at most liquor stores and some gourmet supermarkets. If you cannot find it in your area, substitute 2 shot glasses of vodka and 1½ teaspoon of anise extract.

In a very large mixing bowl, use a hand mixer to whip the vegetable shortening with the oil. Add the sugar and mix until smooth. Add the egg yolks, anise, lemon peel, juice and cinnamon and mix together. Add flour and baking soda to mixture, a cup at a time. Be sure to mix well. Dough should be very smooth and soft.

Preheat oven to 325 °F. Using a teaspoon, scoop out a dollop of dough. Form balls about the size of walnuts, using your hands. If dough is too sticky to roll into balls, mix in additional flour (from ¼-½ cup). Place balls onto ungreased cookie sheet. Lightly press down on each ball to flatten slightly. Using the beaten egg white, brush on the top of each cookie. Bake cookies until they begin to turn light brown on the bottom edges—about 15-20 minutes.

Let the cookies cool 5 minutes before removing from the cookie sheet, as they are very delicate.

~°~°~°~°~°~°~°~°~°~°~°~°~°~°

Gaulettes Cookie

1 pound butter, softened
3 cups light brown sugar
6 eggs
1 tablespoon vanilla
1 teaspoon almond or black walnut extract (optional)
7 cups all-purpose flour
¼ teaspoon baking soda

¼ teaspoon salt

Using a mixer on medium-high speed, cream the butter, brown sugar, eggs, and flavour extracts until the mixture is fluffy. Reduce the mixer speed and stir in the dry ingredients until the dough is completely mixed together.

Preheat a French Belgian waffle iron over medium heat. Place a 1 inch ball of dough into each section of the preheated iron and bake over the medium-heat burner for approximately 45 seconds on each side.

The gullets are done when they turn golden brown. Allow them to cool completely on a wire rack.

This Belgian gullets, or gaulettes, recipe makes approximately 7 dozen cookies.

˷°˷°˷°˷°˷°˷°˷°˷°˷°˷°˷°˷°˷°

Cheddar Granola Cookies

¾ cup (175 ml) all-purpose flour
½ cup (125 ml) whole wheat flour
1 teaspoon (5 ml) each baking soda and salt
½ cup (125 ml) **butter**, softened
½ cup (125 ml) sugar
1/3 cup (75 ml) liquid honey
2 eggs
2 cups (500 ml) granola
2 cups (500 ml) shredded Cheddar cheese
1 ½ cups (375 ml) golden raisins

Preheat oven to 350 °F (180 °C).

In medium bowl, stir together all-purpose flour, whole wheat flour, baking soda and salt.

In large mixer bowl, cream butter until light and fluffy; gradually beat in sugar and honey. Add eggs, one at a time, beating well after each addition. Stir in dry ingredients, granola, Cheddar cheese and raisins; mix well (batter should be stiff).

Drop tablespoons (15 ml) of batter, 1 dozen at a time, about 2 inches (5 cm) apart, onto ungreased baking sheets. With floured fingers, pat into 2 inch (5 cm) circles.

Bake 10 minutes or until lightly browned. Remove from baking sheets immediately; let cool on wire racks.

˷ᵒ ˷ᵒ ˷ᵒ ˷ᵒ ˷ᵒ ˷ᵒ ˷ᵒ ˷ᵒ ˷ᵒ ˷ᵒ ˷ᵒ ˷ᵒ ˷ᵒ

"Nothing is easy to the unwilling."
—Thomas Fuller

Chewy Molasses Sandwich Cookies

2 cups all-purpose flour
1 ½ teaspoons baking soda
½ teaspoon salt
½ teaspoon ground cinnamon
½ teaspoon ground nutmeg
1 cup sugar
¾ cup butter, softened
1 egg
¼ cup molasses
¼ cup sugar
Filling:
2 ½ cups powdered sugar
¼ cup butter, softened
2 tablespoons honey
1 ½ teaspoons freshly grated orange zest
2-3 tablespoons milk

Heat oven to 350 °F. Combine flour, baking soda, salt, cinnamon and nutmeg in medium bowl; set aside.

Combine 1 cup sugar and ¾ cup butter in large bowl. Beat at medium speed until well mixed. Add egg and molasses; continue beating until well mixed. Reduce speed to low; add flour mixture. Beat until well mixed.

Place ¼ cup sugar in small bowl. Shape dough into ¾ inch balls; roll each in sugar. Place 2 inches apart onto ungreased cookie sheets. Bake for 5-7 minutes or until edges are set. (Cookies will have cracks.) Cool 1 minute on cookie sheets; remove to wire cooling rack. Cool completely.

Combine all filling ingredients except milk in small bowl. Beat at low speed until well mixed. Continue beating; adding enough milk for desired filling consistency. Spread bottom-side of 1 cookie with rounded teaspoonful filling; top with another cookie, bottom-side down. Repeat with remaining cookies.

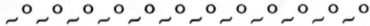

<u>MY SPECIAL RECIPES</u>

Chapter Eight

Squares

—Laughter is brightest where food is best.—
Irish proverb

<u>TIP:</u>
<u>First</u> *rinse raisins, dates and figs in very cold water before putting them through the food chopper. They will not form such a gummy mass.*

<u>Reese Squares</u>

1 ½ cups graham cracker crumbs
1 pound (3-3½ cups) confectioner's sugar
1½ cups peanut butter
1 cup butter, melted
1 (12 ounces) bag milk chocolate chips

Combine graham crumbs, sugar and peanut butter; mix well.
Blend in melted butter until well combined
Press mixture into 9 x 13 inches pan.
Melt chocolate chips; spread over peanut butter mixture.

Chill until set cut into bars.

Black Bean Brownies

1 (15.5 ounces) can black beans, rinsed, drained
3 eggs
3 tablespoons vegetable oil
¼ cup cocoa powder
Pinch salt
1 teaspoon vanilla
¾ cup white sugar
1 teaspoon instant coffee (optional)
½ cup milk chocolate chips (optional)

Preheat oven to 350 °F (175 °C). Lightly grease an 8 x 8 inches square pan. Combine the black beans, eggs, oil, cocoa powder, salt, vanilla, sugar and instant coffee in a blender. Blend until smooth. Pour into baking dish, sprinkle the chocolate chips on the top of mixture. Bake for 30 minutes, until top is dry and edges pull away from pan.

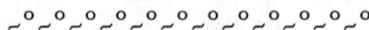

No Bake Rocky Road Bars

10 graham wafers
1 cup semi sweet chocolate chips
½ cup margarine
1 egg
1 cup icing sugar
2 cups multi coloured mini marshmallows
½ cup walnuts, chopped

Line 8 inch square pan with graham wafers; cutting to fit pan. Combine chocolate chips, margarine and egg in saucepan. Stir over medium heat until melted and smooth. Remove from heat. Stir in icing sugar. Cool slightly. Stir in marshmallows. Spread over wafers in pan. Sprinkle with nuts, pressing down gently.

Chill until firm.

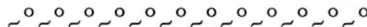

Lemon Squares

1 cup quick oats, uncooked
1 cup flour
½ cup coconut, flaked
½ cup walnuts, coarsely chopped
½ cup brown sugar, firmly packed
1 teaspoon baking powder
½ cup butter or margarine
1 can Eagle Brand sweetened condensed milk
½ cup lemon juice

Preheat oven to 350 °F. In medium bowl, combine oars, flour, coconut, nuts, sugar, baking powder and butter. Stir to form a crumbly mixture. Set aside. In medium bowl combine condensed milk and lemon juice. Put ½ the crumb mixture in a 9 x 9 inches baking pan. Spread sweetened condensed milk mixture on top and sprinkle with remaining crumbs.

Bake 25-30 minutes or until lightly browned.

<u>Lemon Snow bars</u>

1 1/3 + 2 tablespoons cups flour, divided
1 cup sugar, divided
½ cup butter, softened
2 eggs
¼ teaspoon baking powder juice and zest from 1 large lemon*
powdered sugar

Preheat oven to 350 °F. Lightly grease 8 inches square pan. Completely combine 1 1/3 cups flour, ¼ cup sugar and butter. Press down into prepared pan. Bake for 15-20 minutes or until edges are brown. Combine remaining ingredients, except powdered sugar, until well mixed. Pour over crust and continue baking for 18 minutes or until set. Remove from oven and sprinkle with powdered sugar. Cool complete before cutting into 16 bars.

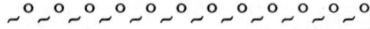

Apple Butter Oat Bars

½ cup flour
1 teaspoon baking soda
1½ teaspoon salt
1 teaspoon cinnamon
1 teaspoon nutmeg
2½ cups rolled oats, uncooked
¾ cup granulated sugar
¾ cup brown sugar
1 cup butter, melted
1 cup apple butter

Preheat oven to 350 °F. Lightly grease 9 x 13 inches pan. Combine first set of ingredients in a large bowl with a wire whisk. Stir in second set of ingredients until combined. Stir in melted butter until crumbly. Sprinkle with ½ mixture into pan. Spread apple butter over mixture in pan. Sprinkle rest of crumbly mixture over apple butter. Bake for 55 minutes. Cool and cut into bars

Eatmore Chocolate Bar

¾ cup honey
1 cup peanut butter, crunchy
12 large or 50 small marshmallows
1 cup chocolate chips
Melt and stir till all dissolved
Add 1 cup salted peanuts
3 cups rice krispies
Pat into 9 x 12 pan. Chill. Cut into squares

Conga Squares

2 cups packed brown sugar
2/3 cup vegetable oil
2 eggs
2 teaspoons vanilla
2 cups all-purpose flour
1 teaspoon baking powder
1 teaspoon baking soda
2 tablespoons water
1 teaspoon salt
2 cups semisweet chocolate chips

1 cup chopped walnuts

In mixing bowl: measure 2 cups brown sugar, vegetable oil, and eggs. Cream on medium for 3 minutes. Add vanilla. Slowly add white flour and baking powder and salt. Add baking soda mixed in hot water separately.

Add chocolate chips, and walnuts if desired. (Or substitute coconut, nuts, or butterscotch chips.)

Pour batter into a 14 x 17 inch pan. Bake for 10 minutes at 400 °F (205 °C) until just golden. Take out of oven just before you think they are done. They cool in the pan. Cut and serve. Try nutmeg and lemon flavouring for variety, reduce lemon to 1 teaspoon.

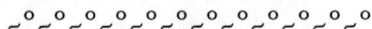

Yum Yum Squares

1½ cups all-purpose flour
2 tablespoons brown sugar
½ cup white sugar
½ cup butter
1½ cups packed brown sugar
2 eggs, beaten
1 cup flaked coconut
½ cup chopped walnuts

Preheat oven to 375 °F (195 °C). Grease a 9 x 9 inches baking pan.

In a medium bowl, mix together the flour, brown sugar, and white sugar. Cut in the ½ cup of butter until mixture resembles coarse crumbs. Pat into the bottom of the prepared pan.

In the same bowl, stir together the eggs and brown sugar, stir in the coconut and walnuts until everything is gooey. Spread evenly over the crust layer, and bake for 25-35 minutes, everything should be golden brown.

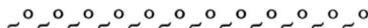

Dream Squares

½ cup butter, softened
½ cup packed brown sugar
½ teaspoon vanilla
1 cup all-purpose flour
2 eggs
1 cup packed brown sugar
1 tablespoon all-purpose flour
½ teaspoon baking powder
Pinch of salt
1 cup chopped walnuts
½ cup candied cherries, quartered
½ cup flaked coconut
1 cup semisweet chocolate chips

Preheat oven to 350 °F (175 °C).

Cream together the butter or margarine with ½ cup of the brown sugar. Stir in the vanilla and the flour. Press this mixture into the bottom of one ungreased 8 x 8 inches square baking pan.

Bake @ 350 °F (175 °C) for 10 minutes.

To Make Topping: Beat the eggs and add 1 cup of the brown sugar. Stir in the 1 tablespoon all purpose flour, the baking powder, pinch salt, chopped walnuts, glace; cherries, coconut and chocolate chips. Spread mixture over the baked pastry.

Return to the oven and bake @ 350 °F (175 °C) for an additional 30-35 minutes or until golden brown. Let cool then cut into squares.

TIP:
When boiling milk, first stir in a pinch of baking soda. This will
help keep the milk from curdling.

~°~°~°~°~°~°~°~°~°~°~°~°~°~°

Chocolate Cream Cheese Brownies

6 ounces semi-sweet chocolate
3 ounces unsweetened chocolate, chopped
2 packages (250g) cream cheese, softened
2 cups white sugar, divided
4 eggs, divided
1 tablespoon vanilla
1 cup butter, room temperature
1 cup all-purpose flour
¼ teaspoon salt

Preheat the oven to 350 °F. Grease a 9 x 13 x 2 inch pan. Combine both the semi-sweet and unsweetened chocolate in a heatproof metal bowl. Place the bowl over a simmering pot of water.

Stir the chocolate occasionally and when completely melted, remove the pot from the heat and set it aside to cool slightly before proceeding.

Place the cream cheese and 1/3 cup of the sugar in a large bowl and beat, until smooth. Beat in 1 egg and 1 teaspoon of vanilla. When completely combined, set aside.

In a separate bowl, beat the butter until light and then add the remaining 1 2/3 cups of sugar until smooth. One at a time add the remaining 3 eggs until well mixed. Add the cooled chocolate and remaining 2 teaspoons of vanilla. When thoroughly combined, mix in the flour and salt.

Reserve 1 cup of the chocolate batter. Spread the remaining batter evenly over the prepared pan. Gently spread the cream cheese mixture over the chocolate batter. Drop the reserved chocolate in dollops over the cream cheese batter. Use the tip of a knife to lightly swirl the chocolate and cream cheese batter. Use the tip of a knife to lightly swirl the chocolate and cream cheese mixture, leaving a marble effect on the top of the batter.

Place the pan on the centre rack of the oven and bake for 35-40 minutes or until done. Cool before slicing.

 ~°~°~°~°~°~°~°~°~°~°~°~°~°~°

Chocolate Nut Bark

1 cup walnuts
1 pound semisweet or bittersweet chocolate, chopped
½ cup pistachios, coarsely chopped
¼ cup dried cranberries

Preheat the oven to 400 °F. Spread the walnuts on a rimmed baking sheet and roast, tossing once, until fragrant 6-8 minutes. Transfer to a cutting board and coarsely chop.

Line a baking sheet with non-stick foil. Melt chocolate in microwaveable bowl on high for 2 minutes. Let stand 1 minute, stir until completely smooth.

Scrape melted chocolate onto the prepared pan and spread into a rectangle (about 14 x 10 inches).

Scatter walnuts, pistachios and cranberries evenly over chocolate. refrigerate until set, about 1 hour. Break into pieces.

 ~°~°~°~°~°~°~°~°~°~°~°~°~°~°

Lemon-coconut Shortbread

Crust:
1 cup all-purpose or rice flour
1 cup coconut, sweetened, shredded
½ cup icing sugar, sifted
½ cup butter, unsalted, room temperature
Filling:
4-5 (1 cup) lemons
6 eggs
2 ¾ cups granulated sugar
½ cup all-purpose or rice flour
Icing sugar for sifting

Preheat oven to 350 °F. Lightly butter a 9 x 13 inches baking dish. In a large bowl, stir flour with coconut and icing sugar to mix. Cut in butter using your fingers or a pastry blender until mixture resembles coarse crumbs. Turn into baking dish and press evenly over bottom. Base will be thin. Bake until crust is golden brown (15-22 minutes). Remove and set aside. Reduce heat to 325 °F.

Filling: Squeeze one cup of juice from lemons into a large bowl. Add eggs and whisk until blended. Stir sugar with flour, then whisk into egg mixture. Pour over hot crust, bake until filling is set when dish is jiggled (30-35 minutes). Set on rack to cool completely.

Cut into squares, sift icing sugar topping as desired.

~°~°~°~°~°~°~°~°~°~°~°~°~°~°

MY SPECIAL RECIPES

Chapter Nine

Misc

"Every now and again take a good look at something not made with hands—a mountain, a star, the turn of a stream. There will come to you wisdom and patience and solace and, above all, the assurance that you are not alone in the world."—Sidney Lovett

<u>TIP:</u>

A copper scouring pad in your humidifier will prevent lime build up.

To remove a stain from inside a glass vase, fill it with water and drop in two Alka-Seltzer tablets.

To remove gum from hair, rub it with peanut butter or cooking oil or between two ice cubes. This will release it.

To remove paint from hands, use lard.

Uses for Toothpaste

1. Relieve irritation from bug bites, sores, and blisters. These skin irritations all tend to weep and, in the case of bug bites, often itch. Apply a drop of toothpaste to a bug bite or insect sting to stop the itching and decrease any swelling. When applied to sores or blisters, it dries them up, thus allowing the wound to heal faster. It's best when used overnight.

2. Soothe a stinging burn. For minor burns that don't involve an open wound, toothpaste can deliver temporary cooling relief. Apply it delicately to the affected area immediately after a burn develops; it temporarily relieves the sting and prevents the wound from weeping or opening.

3. Decrease the size of a facial blemish. Want to speed up the healing of a zit? Apply a tiny dot of toothpaste to the affected area at night before bed. Wash it off in the morning.

4. Clean up your fingernails. Our teeth are made of enamel, and toothpaste is good for them, so it stands to reason that toothpaste would also be good for our fingernails. For cleaner, shinier, and stronger nails, simply scrub the underneath and tops of fingernails with a toothbrush and toothpaste.

5. Keep hair in place. Gel toothpastes contain the same water-soluble polymers that many hair gels are made of. If you're looking to style and hold an extreme hair creation, try gel toothpaste as your go-to product if you're out of regular hair gel. (This is also a great trick for making baby barrettes stay in place.)

6. Scrub away stinky smells. Garlic, fish, onion, and other pungent foods can permeate the skin cells on our hands. Scrubbing hands and fingertips briefly with toothpaste removes all traces of smelly odours

7. Remove stains. Toothpaste can make tough stains on both clothing and carpets disappear. For clothes, apply toothpaste directly to the stain and rub briskly until the spot is gone, then wash as usual. (Note that using a whitening toothpaste on colours can sometimes bleach the fabric.) For carpet stains, apply toothpaste to the stain and scrub it with an abrasive brush, then rinse immediately.

8. Spruce up dirty shoes. This tactic works great on running shoes or scuffed-up leather shoes. As with carpet stains, apply toothpaste directly to the dirty or scuffed area, then scrub with a brush and wipe clean.

9. Remove crayon stains on painted walls. Rub a damp cloth with toothpaste gently on the marked-up wall and watch the Crayola marks disappear.

10. Make silver jewellery and other silver pieces sparkle. Rub toothpaste onto jewellery and leave overnight. Wipe clean with a soft cloth in the morning. Make diamonds shine by giving them a gentle scrub using a toothbrush, toothpaste, and a little water. Rinse thoroughly to remove all traces of toothpaste. Do not use this method on pearls, as it will damage their finish.

11. Remove scratches on DVDs and CDs. This remedy has been used with mixed success rates, but it seems to work fairly well on shallow scratches and smudges. Apply a thin coating of toothpaste to the disc and rub gently, then rinse clean.

12. Tidy up piano keys before tickling them. Piano keys retain oil from the skin, which then attracts dust and dirt. Clean away grime gently with a damp, lint-free cloth and toothpaste; after rubbing in the toothpaste, wipe the keys clean with a second lint-free cloth.

13. Deodorize baby bottles. If baby bottles develop a sour-milk smell, a good cleaning with some toothpaste and a bottle scrubber will clean away residue and deodorize. Always make sure to rinse well.

14. Remove the burned crust on irons. For those of you who still use an iron, you may find that after time, the plate of the iron develops a burned crust. The silica in toothpaste gently grinds away this rusty-looking layer.

15. Defog goggles. Scuba divers, swimmers, and tri-athletes may already know about this handy little trick: Rub a small spot of toothpaste into each lens of your goggles, then rinse thoroughly, and voila! There'll be no need to ever buy expensive defogger gels again. Avoid rubbing too vigorously, though, as the abrasive ingredients in toothpaste could scratch the lenses.

~°~°~°~°~°~°~°~°~°~°~°~°~°~°

Cheesy Soft Pretzels

1½ cups all purpose flour
½ cup cheddar cheese, shredded
2 teaspoons baking powder
1 teaspoon sugar
¾ teaspoon salt
2 tablespoons cold butter or margarine
2/3 cup milk
1 egg, beaten
Coarse salt

In a bowl, combine flour, cheese, baking powder, sugar and salt. Cut in butter until crumbly. Stir in milk just until moistened. Knead on a floured surface for 1 minute; divide in half. Roll each portion into a 12 x 8 inches rectangle; cut each into 8 inch long strips. Fold strips in half, pinching the edges and twist into pretzel shapes. Place on greased baking sheets. Brush with egg and sprinkle with coarse salt.

Bake @ 400 °F for 12-15 minutes or until golden brown.

~°~°~°~°~°~°~°~°~°~°~°~°~°~°

Buttery Soft Pretzels

4 teaspoons active dry yeast
1 teaspoon white sugar
1¼ cups warm water (110 °F, 45 °C)
5 cups all-purpose flour
½ cup white sugar

1½ teaspoons salt
1 tablespoon vegetable oil

½ cup baking soda
4 cups hot water
¼ cup kosher salt, for topping

In a small bowl, dissolve yeast and 1 teaspoon sugar in warm water. Let stand until creamy, about 10 minutes.

In a large bowl, mix together flour, ½ cup sugar, and salt. Make a well in the center; add the oil and yeast mixture. Mix and form into a dough. If the mixture is dry, add one or two tablespoons of water. Knead the dough until smooth, about 7 to 8 minutes. Lightly oil a large bowl, place the dough in the bowl and turn to coat with oil. Cover with plastic wrap and let rise in a warm place until doubled in size, about 1 hour.

Preheat oven to 450 °F (230 °C). In a large bowl, dissolve baking soda in hot water.

When risen, turn dough out onto a lightly floured surface and divide into 12 equal pieces. Roll each piece into a rope and twist into a pretzel shape. Once all of the dough is all shaped, dip each pretzel into the baking soda solution and place on a greased baking sheet.

Sprinkle with kosher salt.

Bake in preheated oven for 8 minutes, until browned.

Soft Pretzel Recipe

For 3 dozen 6-inch sticks or
For 1 dozen 6-inch Pretzels
1 tablespoon yeast
1 tablespoon sugar
1 teaspoon salt

2 tablespoons butter or margarine, softened
1 cup warm (115 °F) water
2¾ cups flour
Coarse Salt to sprinkle on Pretzels before baking
5 tsp baking soda mixed in 4 cups water in a <u>non-aluminum</u> saucepan.
1 large slotted spoon to "go fishing"
Greased cookie sheet
Preheat oven to 475 °F.

Put yeast, sugar, salt, butter, water and ONE CUP of the flour into a medium mixing bowl and pour in the water.

Stir till all smooth, and yeast starts to bubble.

Add the rest of the flour, stir till it is mixed in.

When mixture is too stiff to stir with a spoon, begin kneading.

Knead dough till smooth and till it no longer sticks to the bowl and your hands

Allow dough to rise to about double its height.

While dough is rising, grease the cookie sheet. and prepare the baking soda-water mixture and bring to a boil on stove.

When dough is risen enough, punch down, knead for a minute or so, then divide and roll the 6 inch sticks with your hands, to about ½ inch in diameter, or 12-15 inches long rolls to make into the pretzel shape.

Allow sticks or pretzels to sit for about 1-2 minutes. Place them into boiling water-baking soda mixture one or two at a time.

Let the pretzels boil for 60-70 seconds, then flip them over with the slotted spoon and boil on the other side for 60-70 seconds.

This boiling step gives them a firm skin and adds some flavour. Not boiling long enough leaves them too soft and allows them to rise too much. Boiling too long makes them tough.

Fish them out of the water, let them drip off and place them on the greased cookie sheet.

When all the pretzels or sticks are done, sprinkle the coarse salt on them.

Bake for 12-15 minutes or till sticks or pretzels are golden brown.

 ~°~°~°~°~°~°~°~°~°~°~°~°~°~°~°

Sausage Mushroom Calzones

1 pound sausage
8 ounces fresh mushrooms, chopped
6-8 ounces pizza sauce
1 cup shredded cheese (optional)
1 pound pizza dough (homemade or store bought)

Brown sausage and mushrooms in a large skillet. Drain and place in a bowl to cool. Mix with pizza sauce. Divide pizza dough into four. Roll each ball out into a circle. Place 1/4 of mixture onto each dough circle and add cheese on top if using. Fold circle over and crimp edges using fingers. Bake at 400 °F for 15-20 minutes.

 ~°~°~°~°~°~°~°~°~°~°~°~°~°~°~°

Melting Pancakes

Separate eggs and beat whites until stiff, and set aside. Beat egg yolks with 3 tablespoons flour, pinch salt, 1 cup cottage cheese. Fold whites and yolk mixture together. Drop by large spoonful onto hot greased griddle. Serve.

 ~°~°~°~°~°~°~°~°~°~°~°~°~°~°~°

Rosemary Mushroom Crostini

1 bread
2 tablespoons (30 ml) butter
¼ cup (60 ml) red onion, finely chopped
1 large clove garlic, minced
5 ½ cups (1.375 L) finely chopped mixed mushrooms
¼ cup (60 ml) 35% cream
1 teaspoon (5 ml) minced fresh rosemary
1 cup (250 ml) grated Oka, Emmental or Aged Cheddar cheese
½ cup (125 ml) freshly grated Canadian Parmesan cheese
Salt and freshly ground pepper to taste
Whole pink peppercorns and rosemary

Slice bread into 1/3 inch (1 cm) thick rounds. Toast until golden. Set aside.

Sauté onions and garlic in butter at medium-high for 1 minute. Add mushrooms. Cook 7 minutes, stirring occasionally. Remove from heat.

Stir in cream, rosemary and seasoning. Stir in cheeses. Spread toast with a spoonful of mushroom mixture.

Set on baking sheet and broil until hot (2-3 minutes). Garnish with a few whole pink peppercorns and rosemary. Serve immediately

Mozzarella and Ricotta Calzone

1 ball homemade or store-bought pizza dough (be sure to let dough rise beforehand)
Flour to roll out dough
1/3 cup (50 g) Ricotta cheese
2 cloves garlic, crushed

A few leaves fresh basil (or 1/2 tablespoon /7.5 ml dried basil)

¾ cup (100 g) Mozzarella cheese, grated

2 tablespoons (30 ml) olive oil

4 ounces (125 g) mortadella or prosciutto, chopped

Salt and freshly ground pepper

1 egg, beaten

Preheat oven to 400 °F (200 °C).

Using a rolling pin, roll out dough (it should be quite thin). Using a pastry cutter, cut out circles 10 cms in diameter.

Mix together all ingredients except flour and egg. Season with salt and pepper. Spread mixture in the centre of dough circles. Do not overfill.

Brush egg on dough edges and fold into semicircular pockets. Pinch along edges to seal.

Brush egg over dough pockets, bake in preheated oven 12-15 minutes, until golden. Serve hot.

⁰⁓⁰⁓⁰⁓⁰⁓⁰⁓⁰⁓⁰⁓⁰⁓⁰⁓⁰⁓⁰⁓⁰⁓⁰

Night-Before Cheddar Bagel Casserole

4 plain bagels

1½ cups (375 ml) diced ham

1/2 cup (125 ml) each diced red and green bell peppers

½ cup (125 ml) thinly sliced green onions

2 cups (500 ml) shredded Cheddar cheese

3 tablespoons (45 ml) butter

9 eggs

2½ cups (625 ml) milk

2 tablespoons (30 ml) Dijon mustard

1 teaspoon (5 ml) salt

4 ounces (125 g) Cheddar cheese, thinly sliced

Cut bagels vertically in half. Turn each half moon bagel piece on its side and cut into 6 thin slices. Arrange half the bagel slices in greased 13 x 9 x 2 inch (3.5 L) shallow baking dish.

Combine ham, bell peppers, onions and shredded Cheddar cheese; sprinkle over bagel layer. Butter one side of remaining bagel slices; arrange slices, buttered side up, over cheese mixture.

Whisk together eggs, milk, mustard and salt; pour evenly over bagel mixture. Cover with plastic wrap and refrigerate overnight.

Remove from refrigerator one hour before baking.

Bake uncovered in 350 °F (180 °C) oven one hour or until a knife inserted in centre comes out clean. If top is browning too quickly, cover loosely with foil.

> *"The price of doing the same old thing is far higher than the price of change."*—Bill Clinton

Kentucky Fried Chicken Coating

2 cups flour
1 tablespoon celery salt
2 tablespoons dry mustard
½ tablespoon oregano
1 tablespoon ginger
½ tablespoon sweet basil
1 tablespoon salt
1 tablespoon pepper
4 tablespoons paprika
2 tablespoons garlic salt
½ tablespoon thyme
1 egg
1 cup milk

Combine all ingredients (except egg and milk).

Soak chicken pieces in 1 egg and 1 cup of milk for 1 minute.

Remove and shake in bag of seasoning until well coated.

Bake in 350 °F oven until nice and brown.

Enough coating for 10 pounds of chicken.

<u>MY SPECIAL RECIPES</u>

Wild Rice

TIP:
Add one teaspoon of lemon juice to each quart of water when cooking rice, this will keep rice fluffy.

Wild Rice and Mushroom Soup

½ ounce (½ cup) dried porcini mushrooms
2 cups boiling water
1 to 2 tablespoons extra virgin olive oil, as needed
1 large onion, chopped
2 medium carrots, diced
2 ribs celery, diced
½ pound cremini or button mushrooms, cleaned, trimmed, and sliced thick
2 large garlic cloves, minced
Salt to taste
2/3 cup wild rice
2 quarts chicken stock, vegetable stock, or water

A bouquet garnish made with a few sprigs each thyme and parsley, a bay leaf and a Parmesan rind
1 cup frozen peas, thawed
Freshly ground pepper to taste
Place the dried porcini mushrooms in a bowl or a Pyrex measuring cup, and pour on 2 cups boiling water. Let sit for 30 minutes. Set a strainer over a bowl and line it with cheesecloth. Lift the mushrooms from the water, and squeeze them over the strainer. Rinse in several changes of water, squeeze out the water

and set aside. Pour the soaking water through the cheesecloth-lined strainer, and set aside.

Heat the oil in a large, heavy soup pot or Dutch oven over medium heat. Add the onion, carrot and celery. Cook, stirring often, until just about tender, about five minutes. Add the sliced fresh mushrooms. Cook, stirring, until the mushrooms are beginning to soften, about three minutes. Add the garlic and a generous pinch of salt. Continue to cook for about five minutes until the mixture is juicy and fragrant. Add the reconstituted dried mushrooms, the wild rice, bouquet garnish, mushroom soaking liquid, stock or water, and salt to taste. Bring to a boil, reduce the heat, cover and simmer one hour. Add the peas, and simmer another 10 minutes. Remove the bouquet garnish, taste and adjust salt, add a generous amount of freshly ground pepper and serve.

"Die when I may, I want it said of me by those who knew me best, that I always plucked a thistle and planted a flower where I thought a flower would grow."—Abraham Lincoln

˜°˜°˜°˜°˜°˜°˜°˜°˜°˜°˜°˜°°

Wild Rice Soup

1 medium onion, finely chopped
1 tablespoon butter or margarine
¼ cup flour
4 cups fat-free chicken broth, divided
½ cup carrots, grated or finely chopped
1 can (12 ounces) evaporated fat-free milk
3 cups cooked wild rice*
4 ounces extra lean canned ham, finely diced
2 tablespoons dry sherry
¼ teaspoon nutmeg salt and pepper to taste dash of white pepper to taste

¼ cup slivered almonds, toasted

In a heavy large saucepan, melt butter. Add onion and cook until translucent. In a shaker or jar, combine flour with 1 cup of the broth. Shake or mix until smooth. Add to saucepan along with remaining broth. Bring to a boil while stirring constantly. Boil for 1 minute.

Add carrots and cook until tender. Add milk, cooked rice, ham, sherry, and nutmeg. Heat through and keep warm until ready to serve. Season with salt and pepper.

If soup is too thick, thin with extra broth, milk, or cream.

Serve in individual bowls and top with slivered almonds.

Note: In a large saucepan, cook ¾ cup of wild rice in 6 cups of salted water. Bring to a boil and continue to boil gently for about 45 minutes or until rice is tender. Drain well.

 ˷°˷°˷°˷°˷°˷°˷°˷°˷°˷°˷°˷°˷°

Wild Rice Harvest Casserole

4 cups diced cooked chicken
1 cup chopped celery
2 tablespoons butter or margarine
2 (10.75 ounces) cans condensed cream of mushroom soup, undiluted
2 cups chicken broth
1 (4.5 ounces) can sliced mushrooms, drained
1 small onion, chopped
1 cup uncooked wild rice, rinsed and drained
¼ teaspoon poultry seasoning
¾ cup cashew pieces
Chopped fresh parsley

In a skillet, brown chicken and celery in butter. In a large bowl, combine soup and broth until smooth. Add the mushrooms, onion, rice, poultry seasoning and chicken mixture. Pour into a greased 13 x 9 x 2inches baking dish. Cover and bake @ 350 °F for 1 hour. Uncover and bake for 30 minutes. Stir; sprinkle with cashews.

Return to the oven for 15 minutes or until the rice is tender. Garnish with parsley.

~°~°~°~°~°~°~°~°~°~°~°~°~°~°

Savoury Wild Rice Casserole

3 cups water
1 cup uncooked wild rice
¼ teaspoon salt
1 pound bulk pork sausage
1 medium onion, chopped
1 (14.5 ounces) can chicken broth
1 (10.75 ounces) can condensed cream of chicken soup, undiluted
1 (8 ounces) can mushroom stems and pieces, drained
1 (8 ounces) can sliced water chestnuts, drained
1 teaspoon rubbed sage

In a saucepan, combine water, rice and salt; bring to a boil. Reduce heat; cover and simmer for 55-60 minutes or until rice is tender. Meanwhile, in a skillet, cook sausage and onion until meat is no longer pink; drain. Add broth, soup, mushrooms, water chestnuts, sage and rice. Transfer to a greased 3 quart baking dish.

Bake, uncovered, @ 350 °F for 45-50 minutes or until heated through.

~°~°~°~°~°~°~°~°~°~°~°~°~°~°

"If you don't like something change it; if you can't change it, change the way you think about it."—Mary Engelbreit

<u>MY SPECIAL RECIPES</u>

Chapter Ten

Specialty

"Don't ask yourself what the world needs; ask yourself what makes you come alive. And then go and do that. Because what the world needs is people who have come alive"—Harold Whitman

Quinoa Stir-Fry

2 cups cooked quinoa (cook like rice)
1 cup mushrooms, sliced
½ cup celery, sliced
½ cup carrots, sliced
1 onion, sliced
½ cup cauliflower pieces
1 red pepper, diced
1 cup broccoli, chopped
3 garlic cloves, minced
½ cup sliced almonds
¼ cup sunflower seeds
1 teaspoon seasoning
2 tablespoons teriyaki or soy sauce

Sauté vegetables, garlic, almonds and seeds in sesame oil until vegetables are crisp. Add seasoning and quinoa. Stir until warm and mixed through. Serve immediately.

~°~°~°~°~°~°~°~°~°~°~°~°~°~°~°

Kamut Waffles

1 1/3 cups kamut flour
2/3 cup wheat germ
2 eggs, beaten until fluffy
2 cups milk
6 tablespoons olive oil, virgin
2 teaspoons baking powder

Preheat waffle iron. Spray with non-stick spray.
Combine dry ingredients. Stir together well beaten eggs, milk and oil. Mix with dry ingredients. Add batter to hot waffle iron and cook.

Hint:
Quinoa
Rinse quinoa thoroughly
Bring 1 parts quinoa to 2 parts liquid to boil in a saucepan.
Reduce heat and simmer for 15-18 minutes
Allow to sit covered for 5 minutes.
For variety, try red quinoa!
Liquid Suggestions:
water, chicken broth, vegetable broth, milk, almond milk, soy milk, apple juice, apple cider
Add in Suggestions:
Breakfast:
Oatmeal, sesame seeds, pumpkin seeds, walnuts, pecans, almonds, dried fruits, berries, yogurt, kefir, agave nectar
Lunch and Dinner

Meats: cooked turkey, chicken or sausage
Cheeses: feta, goat cheese, fresh mozzarella, cheddar, swiss
Other: sun dried tomatoes, tomatoes, pine nuts, cilantro, parsley,
chives, roasted garlic, garlic, lemon juice, chipotle peppers, red peppers,
green peppers, jalapenos, dried red pepper flakes, cayenne pepper

Kamut Wild Rice Cranberry Salad

1 cup kamut
1 cup wild rice
1 cup dried cranberries
2 medium carrots, peeled and chopped
1 small red onion, finely chopped
½ cup fresh parsley, finely chopped

Dressing: ½ cup orange juice
¼ cup extra light olive oil
¼ cup red wine vinegar
2 cloves garlic, minced dash Worcestershire sauce
salt and freshly ground pepper to taste

Place kamut in a medium saucepan and cover with water. Soak overnight. Pour off water. Add 1 cup fresh water. Bring to a boil. Cover, reduce heat, and simmer for 50-60 minutes or until tender. (Most of the water should be absorbed.) Remove from heat and cool.

Wash wild rice and place in a medium saucepan with 3 cups of water. Bring to a boil. Cover, reduce heat and boil gently for 40-50 minutes or until tender. (Do not over-cook, which makes the rice mushy.) Remove from heat and drain off any remaining liquid. Cool. In a large bowl, combine kamut, rice, dried cranberries, carrots, onions, and parsley. Set aside.

In a pint jar, combine all of the dressing ingredients. Mix well and pour over rice mixture. Stir to mix well. Cover and refrigerate until ready to serve.

"Let go of the past and go for the future. Go confidently in the direction of your dreams. Live the life you imagined."—Henry David Thoreau

Sunflower Crackers

1 cup cracked wheat flour
¼ cup quinoa flour
¼ cup buckwheat flour
¼ cup wheat germ
¼ cup ground flax
½ teaspoon salt
6 tablespoons sunflower seeds (blend seeds in food processor)
6-8 tablespoons olive oil
10-12 tablespoons water

Combine the first 7 ingredients, add oil and water adding first enough to form a soft dough. Knead and roll on floured surface to approximately inch thickness. Cut with cookie cutter or glass tumbler. Bake for 10 minutes. You may prick with a fork before baking.

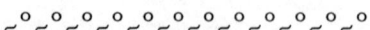

Quinoa Waffles

1 cup quinoa flour
1¼ cups white flour
4 teaspoons baking powder
¾ teaspoons salt
1½ tablespoons sugar

2 eggs, beaten
2¼ cups milk
½ cup salad oil

Sift together dry ingredients. Combine remaining ingredients and add just before baking, beat until only moistened. Batter will be thin. Bake in pre—heated waffle iron. Makes 10-12 waffles. The quinoa flour adds a nutty flavour and the waffles stay fresh longer than made with regular flour. If you are a celiac or are on a gluten-free diet, the pancakes can be made with 100% quinoa flour (2¼ cups) for a delicious breakfast treat.

₀˷₀˷₀˷₀˷₀˷₀˷₀˷₀˷₀˷₀˷₀˷₀˷₀˷₀

Bread Sticks (Gluten Free)

Gluten-Free baking mix:
4 cup quinoa flour
1 1/3 cup potato starch flour
2/3 cup tapioca starch flour
1 tablespoon instant yeast
1 - 1¼ cup warm water
tablespoon sugar
¼ - ½ teaspoon salt
1 -1½ tablespoons olive oil
1 egg
2 cup quinoa flour
2 teaspoons xanthan gum
3 tablespoon dry milk powder
1 cup gluten free baking mix

Egg Wash:
1 egg
1 tablespoon water
pinch of salt

233

Beat egg, salt and water together.

Mix together the sugar, salt, olive oil, egg, and ¾ cup warm water. Mix the flours, instant yeast, xanthan gum, sugar, salt, dry milk powder together. Mix the dry ingredients with wet mixture and blend to form a dough. Add enough of the remaining water, so dough just sticks together but is not dry. Turn dough out onto a lightly floured surface. Knead by hand a minute or two until the dough feels smooth and no longer feels tacky to touch.

Flouring your hands, divide dough into approximately 20 pieces. Roll each small piece of dough to form a pencil-like stick. Make the sticks 10-12 inches long and about ½ inch in diameter. Smooth each stick as you work. Repeat until all the dough pieces are shaped into bread sticks. Place bread sticks on greased baking sheet about 2 inches apart. Cover lightly with plastic wrap that has been sprayed with vegetable oil on one side. Allow to rise in a warm place until doubled. Gently brush the egg wash on each bread stick. Bake bread sticks in oven at 400 °F for about 12 minutes or until sticks are crusty and brown.

Quinoa—Basic Recipe

1 cup Quinoa
1 cup boiling water

Place Quinoa in a 1½ quart saucepan of boiling water. Bring to a boil and simmer 8-10 minutes. Cook until all of the water is absorbed. Add more boiling water if necessary to ensure Quinoa does not boil dry. Fluff the cooked Quinoa with a fork and serve with butter, soya sauce or use in recipes calling for cooked Quinoa. Increase the amount of water to use as a breakfast cereal, if a thicker consistency is desired.

Toasted Quinoa Salad

¾ cup Quinoa, uncooked
1 cup diced carrots
½ cup red bell pepper, chopped
¼ cup parsley, minced
2 green onions, sliced
1 lemon, squeezed or (1 - 2 tablespoons juice)
1 lime, squeezed or (1 - 2 tablespoons juice)
1½ tablespoons soy sauce or tamari
2 cloves garlic, minced
1 teaspoon chili sauce (tabasco)

Rinse Quinoa and drain. Put in a pot and dry toast until a few grains begin to pop. Add 1½ cups water, bring to a boil, cover and simmer for 15 minutes, or until the Quinoa has absorbed all the liquid. Remove from heat and let stand for 10 minutes. Fluff with fork and let cool.

Mix carrot, red pepper, parsley and green onion in large bowl. Add cooled Quinoa and toss to combine. Whisk together lemon and limejuices, Soya sauce or tamari, garlic and chili sauce. Pour over salad and combine well. Chill until serving time. We also enjoy throwing in a few steamed, cooled snow peas.

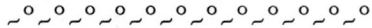

Quinoa and Wild Rice

1 cup Wild Rice
1 cup Quinoa
1/3 cup bacon, chopped
½ cup celery
1 onion, chopped

1 cup mushrooms, sliced

    Cook Wild Rice in 4 cups boiling water about 1 hour until all water has been absorbed

    During the last 15 minutes, add Quinoa and, if rice is almost dry, 1 additional cup of boiling water

    While rice is cooking, fry the bacon in a pan. When crisp, remove and drain

    Mix vegetables and bacon with rice and Quinoa mixture in a casserole dish. Microwave on high for 10 minutes; or in the oven at 350 °F for ½ hour.

꙾ ꙾ ꙾ ꙾ ꙾ ꙾ ꙾ ꙾ ꙾ ꙾ ꙾

<u>Meatless Quinoa Burgers</u>

2 cups cooked Quinoa
1 onion, chopped
1 carrot, grated
1 clove garlic, minced
1 tablespoon onion soup mix or preferred seasonings
½ cup bread crumbs
1 celery stalk, finely chopped
1 egg (beaten) - This makes a firmer burger

    Mix above ingredients, add salt and pepper to taste. Form burger with wet hands (patties are about 4 inches in diameter and ½ inch thick. Lightly oil frying pan. Cook about 5 minutes each side until golden brown.

Variations:
½ cup cooked and finely chopped broccoli
½ cup mushrooms, finely chopped

꙾ ꙾ ꙾ ꙾ ꙾ ꙾ ꙾ ꙾ ꙾ ꙾ ꙾

Minestrone-Quinoa Soup

2 tablespoons olive oil
½ cup green pepper
2 tablespoons butter
½ cup celery
1 large onion, chopped
½ cup carrot, diced
1 clove garlic, minced
pinch of thyme
2 tablespoons parsley
1 teaspoon dried basil
6 cups chicken stock
1 bay leaf
10 ounces tomatoes
2 cups shredded cabbage
1 cup kidney beans (canned or cooked)
½ cup elbow macaroni or pasta
½ - 1 cup Quinoa (depending on desired thickness)
Optional: ½ cup Parmesan cheese sprinkled on top

Heat oil and butter, add onion, garlic and chopped vegetables. Cook until softened.

Add spices, parsley and pinch of salt. Stir in stock and chopped tomatoes. Bring to a boil and simmer 10 minutes.

Add cabbage, beans, macaroni and Quinoa. Cover and simmer ½ hour.

_°_°_°_°_°_°_°_°_°_°_°_°_°_°_°

Tabbouleh (Tabouli)

This middle eastern salad is excellent with fresh summer ripe tomatoes. The mint makes it excellent.

3 cups cooked Quinoa, cooled
1 large tomato
1 cup fresh parsley
1 large cucumber
1 green pepper
½ cup green onions or red onion, diced finely

Dressing:
½ cup lemon juice
2 teaspoons minced garlic
½ cup olive oil
1 teaspoon pepper and salt
Optional: ½ - 1 cup fresh mint or 2 tablespoons dried

Combine Quinoa with pepper, parsley and onion
Mix dressing ingredients together in separate bowl. Add to Quinoa mixture. Add tomato and cucumber
Let sit for 30 minutes to allow flavors to blend.

~°~°~°~°~°~°~°~°~°~°~°~°

Quinoa Chili

1 onion, chopped
1 teaspoon chili powder
1 (796 ml) can tomatoes, diced
1 can tomato sauce or soup
1 can kidney beans
1 pound hamburger
1 teaspoon garlic powder

½ - 1 cup Quinoa (depending on desired consistency)

Fry onion in a pan and brown hamburger

To browned hamburger add chili powder, garlic powder and, if desired, other spices of your choice (cayenne pepper, etc.).

Mix in tomato sauce and canned tomatoes. Add kidney beans and simmer for 15 minutes. Add uncooked Quinoa to chili and cook for another 10-15 minutes, stirring every few minutes

NOTE: Quinoa is a natural and nutritional thickener for soups, stews and casseroles.

~°~°~°~°~°~°~°~°~°~°~°~°~°~°~°

Quinoa Hamburger Buns (Gluten Free)

½ cup water
2 teaspoons sugar
1½ tablespoons dry yeast

Dissolve the 2 teaspoons of sugar in ½ cup lukewarm water. Sprinkle yeast on top and let sit 10 minutes until it starts foaming.

¼ cup canola oil
1 teaspoon vinegar
3/4 cup water
Mix oil with vinegar and ¾ cup water
3 large eggs
1/3 cup sugar (less the 2 tsp above)
1½ teaspoons salt
2/3 cup non-fat dry milk
2 cup quinoa flour
2 cup tapioca flour
3 ½ teaspoons xanthan gum

Sift together dry ingredients. Stir in the yeast mixture and the oil/vinegar mixture into the dry ingredients. Then add eggs and beat for 2 minutes with the mixer on high.

With a large serving spoon or an ice cream scoop, spoon like drop biscuits onto greased cookie sheet. Let rise in a warm oven for 20 to 30 minutes. Bake at 350 °F for 15 to 20 minutes.

Quinoa Spoon Bread (Nachinka)

1 small onion, chopped
1 cup Quinoa
1 teaspoon sugar
4 eggs, well-beaten
1 teaspoon baking soda
¼ pound butter or margarine
1 teaspoon salt
1 quart warm milk
1 teaspoon cinnamon

Fry the chopped onion in butter until golden brown. Turn the heat to low. Add Quinoa right out of the package into the butter and mix well. Add the sugar, salt and warm milk. Stir slowly until the quinoa starts to thicken.

Remove from heat. Add the well-beaten eggs and baking soda and cinnamon. Mix well and place in a casserole dish. Bake in a 325 °F oven for 1 hour.

Banana Cake Quinoa

Topping:
½ cup nuts, chopped
½ cup sugar
1 teaspoon cinnamon
Cake:
2½ cups Quinoa, cooked
2 cups brown sugar
¾ cup vegetable oil
½ cup sour milk or buttermilk
1 tablespoon baking soda
3 eggs
4 cups Oatmeal
3 cups white flour
2 teaspoons cinnamon
2 teaspoons baking powder
4 bananas, mashed
½ cup nuts, chopped
1 teaspoon cinnamon
½ cup sugar

Beat together the sugar, milk, oil and eggs. Add the Quinoa. Combine oatmeal and bananas. Mix well. Add to Quinoa mixture. Combine flour, baking soda, baking powder and cinnamon. Add to Quinoa mix. Pour into a 9 x 13 inches cake pan or 24 muffin cups and sprinkle with mixed topping ingredients.

Bake at 350 °F for 40 minutes ~cake, 20 minutes muffins.

~°~°~°~°~°~°~°~°~°~°~°~°~°~°

Delicate Maple Quinoa Squares

Bottom Layer:
½ cup butter or margarine
1½ cups Quinoa Flour
¼ cup icing sugar
1 teaspoon maple flavouring

Mix the above ingredients together and pat into a 9 inch square pan. Bake in pre-heated 350 °F oven for 15 minutes.

Top Layer:
¾ cup sugar
2 eggs
2 tablespoons Quinoa Flour
½ teaspoon baking powder
2 tablespoons maple flavouring

Combine above ingredients and pour over warm, baked bottom layer. Bake at 350 °F for 25 minutes. While they're still warm, sprinkle with icing sugar. Cut into small squares. Variation: Omit maple flavouring and substitute 1 tsp butter flavouring and 1 tsp rum flavouring and rum flavouring for bottom layer.

˷°˷°˷°˷°˷°˷°˷°˷°˷°˷°˷°˷°˷°

Quinoa Flax Muffins

1½ cups Quinoa flour
1 cup rice flour
½ cup tapioca flour
1 teaspoon baking soda
1 teaspoon baking powder
1 teaspoon salt
2 teaspoons cinnamon

½ cup milled flax seed
1 cup walnuts, chopped
½ cup raisins or cranberries
1 cup carrots, finely grated
1 cup pineapple, crushed or apples, shredded
2 large eggs
1 cup brown sugar
1 cup rice or soy milk
1 teaspoon vanilla
4 tablespoons vegetable oil or margarine

Preheat oven to 375 °F. Thoroughly mix first 7 ingredients together and set aside.

In a separate bowl, cream oil with brown sugar. Add eggs, milk and vanilla. Stir in dry and remaining ingredients. Stir only till mixed. Do Not Over-mix.

Fill muffin cups till full. Bake @ 375 °F for 30-35 minutes or until centres are dry.

~°~°~°~°~°~°~°~°~°~°~°~°~°

<u>MY SPECIAL RECIPES</u>

<u>Celiac</u>

"Failure is not fatal, but failure to change might be."—John Wooden

TIP:

General Baking Mixes:		
Simple Substitute	makes 1 cup	1 cup brown rice flour
General Baking	makes 2 cups	1 cup rice flour ½-¾ cup potato starch ¼ cup tapioca starch/flour
General Baking	makes 9 cups	3 cups garfava bean flour 2 cups potato starch 2 cups cornstarch 1 cup tapioca flour 1 cup sorghum flour

Original formula	makes 3 cups	2 cups rice flour 2/3 cup potato starch 1/3 cup tapioca starch/flour
Four Flour Bean	makes 3 cups	2/3 cup garfava bean flour 1/3 cup sorghum flour 1 cup cornstarch 1 cup tapioca starch/flour
Feather-light	makes 3 cups	1 cup rice flour 1 cup cornstarch 1 cup tapioca starch/flour 1 Tbsp. potato flour
Specialty Mixes:		
Pastry mix	makes 1 cup	1/8 cup potato flour 7/8 cup Ener-G Foods© rice flour
Cookie mix	makes 2 cups	¼ cup chickpea flour 1¾ cup sorghum flour ¼ cup sweet rice flour

Bread mix	makes 2 cups	1 cup brown rice flour ½ cup potato starch ½ cup sweet rice flour 1 Tbsp. unflavoured gelatin

<u>*Gluten-free self-rising flour:*</u>
2 tablespoons potato flour enough white rice flour to make it up to 1 cup
1/2 teaspoon bicarbonate soda
1/2 teaspoon cream of tartar
1 teaspoon xanthan gum OR guar gum
OR pre-gel starch
Gluten-free baking powder:
1/4 cup bicarbonate soda (baking soda)
1/2 cup cream of tartar
Mix well and keep in an airtight container.

Flour combinations:
The following combinations of flours work well together:

2 cups rice flour, 2/3 cup potato flour, 1/3 cup tapioca flour.
2 cups white rice flour, 2/3 cup potato starch flour, 1/3 cup tapioca flour and a teaspoon of xanthan gum.
½ soya flour and ½ cornstarch.
½ soya flour and ½ potato flour.
½ soya flour and ½ rice flour.
½ soya flour, ¼ potato flour, ¼ rice flour.

Note: When buying soy flour, look for debittered soya flour. It has a milder flavour. Plain full fat soy flour has a noticeable stronger flavour.

Gluten-free pastry:
This is good for sweet pies, tarts and cheesecakes.
60g (2oz) cornstarch (maize corn flour)
3/4 cup non-instant dry milk powder
1½ cups coconut
120g (4oz) melted butter
Simply mix and press into a dish. This isn't exactly pastry, so don't roll it.

To replace the gluten:

If you simply take gluten out of your baking, you're likely to have disappointing results. Gluten is sticky stuff which helps prevent your baked goodies from crumbling. It also traps pockets of air, improving the texture of your bread, cakes or biscuits.

Bakers replace it with xanthan gum, guar gum, or pre-gel starch. Xanthan gum is a natural product made from Xanthomonas campestris. This microorganism is grown in the lab for its cell coat, which is dried and ground to form xanthan gum. Xanthan gum is added as a powder to the dry bread ingredients. One teaspoon is needed for every cup of gluten-free flour. You can buy this product at your local health food. You can also use Guar Gum, a vegetable gel, which is cheaper than Xanthan gum.

Gluten-free Flour Mix:
2 cups rice or millet flour
2/3 cup potato starch
1/3 cup tapioca flour
1-2 tsp. of xanthan gum

Each type of flour acts a little differently in relation to other ingredients in a recipe. Many recipes depend on wheat flour for their texture or rising power, so you may have to experiment a bit to see which flours work best when interchanged. To start, change 1/4 of the flour or less. The chart below will give you a good starting point.

You can make your own flour from oatmeal or other rolled grains in a blender or food processor. Use 1½ cups oats to make about 1 cup oat flour. Potato and soy flours are best used in combination with other flours. They have a strong flavour and soy flour has a darker coloring. Rice flour gives a distinctively grainy texture to baked products. Rye flour is frequently used although it has a dark color and distinctive flavour. (Barley, oat, and rye flours all contain some gluten.)

Wheat Flour Substitutions
per cup

Grain (Flour)	Amount
Barley	1 1/4 cups
Cornmeal	1 cup
Corn flour	1 cup
Oat	1 1/3 cups
Potato	3/4 cup
Rice	3/4 cup
Rye	1 1/3 cups
Soy	1 1/3 cups
Tapioca	1 cup

The Gluten-Free Diet:

Foods Allowed:

- Amaranth
- Arrowroot flour
- Baking soda Bean flour Buckwheat
- Cassava (Manioc flour)
- Chick pea flour
- Corn flour
- Cornmeal
- Cornstarch (Masa farina)
- Cream of tartar
- Dal or Dahl (Legume from India)
- Flax
- Gelatin
- Green pea flour
- Gums:
  - o Acacia (Gum Arabic)
  - o
  - Carob bean gum
  - o Carrageenan
  - o Cellulose
  - o Guaica
  - o Guar
- Malto dextrin
- Maltol (A sweetener not related to malt)
- Maltose
- Mannitol
- Millet
- Molasses
- Mustard flour (ground mustard)
- Oats* (pure uncon-taminated)
- Poi
- Potato flour
- Potato starch
- Quinoa
- Rice bran
- Rice flour
- Rice flour (glutinous, sweet)
- Rice polishings
- Rice starch
- Sorghum
- Soya flour
- Soya starch
- Spices
- Sweet potato
- Tapioca flour

o Karaya o Locust bean o Tragacanth o Xanthum • Invert Sugar • Kudzu • Lecithin • Legumes: Seeds of plants which include o Channa o Chick peas o Gram o Lentils o Peanuts o Peas o Soya	• Tapioca starch • Teff • Tofu • White vinegar • Xanthum gum • Yam • Yeast

Foods to Question:

Milk Products	Milk Drinks	Chocolate milk and other flavoured drinks may con-tain wheat starch or barley malt
	Cheese Spreads or Sauces (e.g. Nacho)	May be thick-ened/stabilized with wheat. Flavourings and season-ings may contain wheat.

	Flavoured or frozen yogurt	May be thick-ened/stabilized with a glu-ten source. May contain granola or cookie crumbs
	Sour Cream	Some low-fat/fat-free may contain modified food starch mixed with wheat flour.
Grains	Buckwheat Flour	Pure buckwheat flour is gluten-free. Sometimes buckwheat flour may be
	Rice Cereals	May contain barley malt extract.
	Corn Cereals	May contain oat syrup or barley malt extract.
	Buckwheat Pasta	Some "soba" pastas con-tain pure buckwheat flour which is gluten-free but others may also contain wheat flour.
	Rice Cakes, Corn Cakes, Rice Crackers	Multigrain often contains barley and/or oats Some contain soy sauce (may be made from wheat)
	Oats**	Only use pure uncontaminated oats

Meats/ Alternatives	Baked Beans	Some are thickened with wheat flour
	Imitation Crab	May contain fillers made from wheat starch
	Dry Roasted Nuts	May contain wheat
	Processed Meat Products	May contain fillers made from wheat. May contain HPP or HVP made from wheat.
	Imitation Meats	Often contain wheat or oats.
	Dried Fruits	Dates and other dried fruits may be dusted wheat flour to prevent sticking.
	Fruits/Veg's with sauces Fruit Pie Fillings	Some may be thickened with flour.
	French Fries	May contain wheat as an ingredient. Also may have been cooked in oil also used for battered products.
	Canned Soups, Dried Soup Mixes, Soup bases and Bouillon Cubes	

	Salad Dressings	Seasonings may contain wheat flour or wheat starch.
	Milk Puddings/ Mixes	Starch source may be from wheat.
	Beverages	Some instant teas, herbal teas, coffee substitutes and other drinks may have grain additives. Non-dairy substitutes (e.g., rice drinks and soy drinks) may contain barley, barley malt extract or oats.
	Lemon Curd	Some potato chips contain wheat. Seasoning mixtures may contain wheat flour, wheat starch or hydrolysed wheat protein.
	Baking Powder	Contains starch which may be from wheat.
	Seasonings, Seasoning Mixes	May contain wheat flour, wheat starch or hydrolysed wheat protein.
	Worcestershire Sauce	May contain malt vinegar which is not gluten-free.

Foods to Avoid:
GLUTEN-CONTAINING INGREDIENTS TO BE AVOIDED

Barley	Graham Flour	Rye
Bulgar	Kamut*	Semolina
Cereal Binding	Malt**	Spelt (Dinkel)*
Couscous	Malt Extract**	Triticale
Durum*	Malt Flavouring**	Wheat
Einkorn*	Malt Syrup**	Wheat Bran
Emmer*	Oats***	Wheat Germ
Filler	Oat Bran***	Wheat Starch
Farro*	Oat Syrup***	

* Types of Wheat
** Derived from barley

> *Happiness is not in our circumstances but in ourselves. It is not some-thing we see, like a rainbow, or feel, like the heat of a fire. Happiness is something we are."—John B. Sheerin*

No-Bake Church Window Cookies

5 ounces (142 g) bittersweet chocolate, chopped
3 ounces (85 g) milk chocolate, chopped
¼ cup (50 ml) butter
¼ cup (50 ml) whipping cream
½ cup (125 ml) icing sugar
3 cups (750 ml) mini fruit-flavoured marshmallows
1½ cups (375 ml) unsweetened coconut, shredded
½ cup (12n ml) walnuts, chopped

In large heatproof bowl over saucepan of hot water, melt together bittersweet and milk chocolate, butter and cream until smooth. Stir in icing sugar until smooth. Fold in marshmallows,

½ cup (125 ml) of the coconut and walnuts. Refrigerate for 15 minutes.

Divide into thirds. Using plastic wrap, roll each firmly into a log 8 inches long. Refrigerate until firm.

Let logs stand at room temperature for 5 minutes. Roll in remaining coconut. Cut each log into 12 pieces.

Juicy Meatloaf

1½ pounds lean ground beef
¼ cup onion, chopped
¼ cup bell pepper, chopped
¼ cup quick cooking, gluten free oats
1/8 cup yellow cornmeal
1 cup gluten free, dried bread crumbs
1½ teaspoon salt
1 tablespoon confectioner's sugar
1 egg, beaten
½ cup tomato juice
½ cup water
1 tablespoon gluten free BBQ sauce
Liquid smoke
1 tablespoon white vinegar
¼ cup ketchup
1 tablespoon brown sugar
2 teaspoons yellow mustard

Preheat oven to 350 °F. In a large bowl, combine the beef, onion, pepper oatmeal, cornmeal, bread crumbs, salt, sugar, egg, tomato juice, water, BBQ sauce, 1/8 teaspoon liquid smoke and vinegar.

Mix together thoroughly and place mixture into a lightly greased 9 x 5 inches loaf pan. In separate bowl, combine the ketchup, brown sugar, mustard and 2 drops liquid smoke and mix thoroughly. Spread over the top of the meatloaf. Bake @ 350 °F for 1 hour.

~°~°~°~°~°~°~°~°~°~°~°~°~°~°

*"So long as a person is capable of self-renewal
they are a living being."*
—Henri-Frederic Amiel

Pumpkin Streusel Cheesecake Bars

1 box gluten free yellow cake mix
½ cup pecans, finely chopped
½ cup butter, softened
2 packages (8 ounces) cream cheese, softened
1 cup sugar
1 cup canned pumpkin
1 tablespoon pumpkin pie spice
2 tablespoons whipping cream
2 eggs

Heat oven to 350 °F. In medium bowl, stir together cake mix and pecans. Cut in butter until mixture is crumbly. Reserve 1 cup of mixture for topping. In bottom of ungreased 9 x 13 inches pan, press remaining mixture. Bake 10 minutes.

In large bowl, beat cream cheese and sugar until smooth. Add remaining ingredients, beat until smooth. Pour over warm crust. Sprinkle with reserved topping.

Bake about 35 minutes or until center is set.

Beef and Broccoli Noodle Bowl

8 ounces gluten free wide noodles
3 cups broccoli florets
12 ounces top sirloin steak, cubed
1 medium onion, cut into ½ inch slices
2 cloves garlic, minced
1 tablespoon vegetable oil
1 tablespoon gluten free flour
Salt and pepper to taste
15 ounces beef broth
¼ cup tomato paste
1 teaspoon horseradish

Cook noodles as per directions, add broccoli the last 3 minutes of cooking; drain and keep warm. Trim fat from beef. In a large skillet cook beef, onion and garlic until onion is tender and beef is desired doneness. Sprinkle flour, salt and pepper over meat. Stir to coat. Add beef broth, tomato paste and horseradish to beef. Cook and stir until thickened and bubbly; cook and stir 1 minute more. Divide noodle mixture between four bowls; spoon beef mixture on top. Serve.

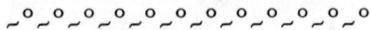

Gluten Free Buttermilk Biscuits

½ cup potato starch
¾ cup cornstarch
1 ¾ teaspoons xanthan gum
1 tablespoon baking powder
¼ teaspoon baking soda
½ teaspoon salt
1 tablespoon salt
1/3 cup cold butter, ¼ inch cubed
¾ cup buttermilk

Preheat oven to 375 °F. Spray baking sheet with cooking spray.

Place the starches, xanthan gum, baking powder, baking soda, salt and sugar into the bowl. Mix.

Sprinkle the butter cubes evenly over the flour mixture. Blend, the mixture should resemble coarse crumbs. Pour the buttermilk evenly over the mixture. Blend until the dough gathers into a moist clump. Break into biscuit shapes and place on baking sheet. Note: try not to handle dough too much. Bake.

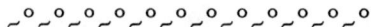

Basic Tomato Sauce

2 tablespoons olive oil
½ medium onion, finely chopped
1 small carrot or 1/2 large carrot, finely chopped
1 small stalk of celery, including the green tops, finely chopped
2 tablespoons chopped fresh parsley
1 clove garlic, minced
1/2 teaspoon dried basil or 2 tablespoons chopped fresh basil
1 (28 ounces) can whole tomatoes, including the juice, or 1¾ pounds fresh tomatoes, peeled, seeded, and chopped
1 teaspoon tomato paste
Salt and freshly ground black pepper to taste

Heat olive oil in a large wide skillet on medium heat. Add the chopped onion, carrot, celery and parsley. Stir to coat. Reduce the heat to low, cover the skillet and cook for 15-20 minutes, stirring occasionally until the vegetables are softened and cooked through.

Remove cover and add the minced garlic. Increase the heat to medium high. Cook for garlic for 30 seconds. Add the tomatoes, including the juice and shredding them with your fingers if you are using canned whole tomatoes. Add the tomato paste and the basil. Season with salt and pepper to taste. Bring to a low simmer, reduce the heat to low and cook, uncovered until thickened, about 15 minutes. If you want you can push the sauce through a food mill, or blend it with an immersion blender, to give it a smooth consistency.

Makes 2½ cups of sauce.

~°~°~°~°~°~°~°~°~°~°~°~°~°

"Faced with the choice between changing one's mind and proving that there is no need to do so, almost everyone gets busy on the proof."
—John Kenneth Galbraith

Beef Stew with Mushrooms and White Beans

1¼ pounds boneless beef top sirloin steak, cut ¾ inch cubes
1 tablespoon olive oil
½ teaspoon salt
¼ teaspoon pepper
1½ teaspoons olive oil
2 medium carrots, cut into ¼ inch thick slices
2 small onions, each cut lengthwise into 8 wedges
8 ounces of cremini or button mushrooms, quartered
1/4 cup dry white wine
1 (16-ounces) can small white beans, rinsed, drained
1 (14½ ounces) can diced tomatoes with garlic and onion, undrained

In a large skillet, heat 1 tablespoon olive oil over medium-high heat. Stir-fry the beef cubes in two batches, 1-2 minutes each, or until the outside is no longer pink. Remove from skillet and season with salt and pepper.

In the same skillet, heat 1½ teaspoons olive oil over medium heat until hot. Add carrots, stir-fry for 3 minutes, then add the onions and stir-fry 5-8 minutes more, until crisp-tender. Stir in mushrooms and wine. Continue stir-frying 5 minutes. Stir in beans and tomatoes. Continue cooking 3 more minutes.

Return the cooked beef to the skillet. Cook 2 minutes more until just heated through.

~°~°~°~°~°~°~°~°~°~°~°~°~°~°

Berry and Banana Terrine

2 envelopes (1/4 ounce each) unflavoured gelatin
2 cups white grape juice
½ cup sugar
5½-6 cups of mixed fresh berries and slices of banana (berries can include boysenberries, strawberries, blueberries, raspberries, and blackberries)

In a small bowl, sprinkle gelatin over ¼ cup grape juice; let soften 2-3 minutes.

Heat sugar with another 1/4 cup grape juice in a small saucepan over medium-high heat until dissolved. Remove from heat; stir in softened gelatin until dissolved, then stir in remaining 1½ cups grape juice.

Place berries in a 4 x 8 inches (6 cup capacity) loaf pan; pour gelatin mixture over, pressing berries gently to submerge completely (remove a few berries if necessary.) Refrigerate until firm, at least 3 hours.

To unmold, dip bottom of pan in hot water about 5 seconds. Invert onto a serving platter, and shake firmly to release. Slice to serve.

Serve with whipped cream. Serves 6-8.

263

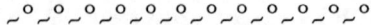

<u>Flaky Buttermilk Biscuits</u>

Also known as baking soda biscuits, these buttery morsels are delicious on their own or can be used to make the perfect gluten-free strawberry shortcakes.

1 cup tapioca flour
½ cup sweet white rice flour
½ cup white rice flour
½ cup potato starch
½ cup cornstarch
1½ teaspoons xanthan gum
4 teaspoons baking powder
1½ teaspoons baking soda
1 teaspoon sugar
1 teaspoon salt
5 tablespoons vegetable shortening
4 tablespoons cold unsalted butter, cut into bits
1½ cups buttermilk

Preheat the oven to 425 °F. Grease a baking sheet.

In a medium bowl, combine the tapioca flour, sweet rice flour, white rice flour, potato starch, cornstarch, xanthan gum, baking powder, baking soda, sugar and salt. Stir with a whisk to blend.

Using your fingers, a pastry blender, or two dinner knives, rub or cut the shortening and butter into the dry ingredients until the mixture is coarse and crumbly. Add the buttermilk and stir just until the dry ingredients are moistened.

Drop ¼-cup mounds of dough 2 inches apart on the prepared pan. Bake for 10 to 12 minutes or until golden brown. Remove from the oven and let cool slightly. Serve warm.

~°~°~°~°~°~°~°~°~°~°~°~°~°~°

Blueberry Cinnamon Scones

2¾ cups brown rice flour
1½ cups + 1 tablespoon garbanzo bean flour
1 teaspoon baking powder
½ teaspoon baking soda
¾ teaspoon sea salt
1 teaspoon ground cinnamon
1 cup canola oil
1 cup organic whole cane sugar
1 cup rice milk
¾ cup frozen blueberries

Combine the brown rice flour, garbanzo bean flour, baking powder, baking soda, salt and cinnamon in a large bowl. In the bowl of a standing mixer fitted with the paddle attachment, combine the canola oil and organic whole cane sugar until well mixed. With the mixer on low speed, add the flour mixture and rice milk alternately, a little at a time, until well mixed, about 3 minutes. Chill the dough for at least 3 hours or overnight.

Preheat the oven to 375 °F.

Dust your counter liberally with brown rice flour. Knead the blueberries into the chilled dough and pat the dough into a 2-inch thick disc. Cut the disc into 8 wedges. Place the wedges onto a greased or parchment-line baking sheet, spaced evenly apart. Bake until scones are golden brown and firm to the touch, about 30 minutes.

~°~°~°~°~°~°~°~°~°~°~°~°~°~°

MY SPECIAL RECIPES

Lactose Intolerant

People change and forget to tell each other.
—Lillian Hellman

Ham Cabbage Potato Skillet

2 tablespoons margarine
1 onion, chopped
1 small head cabbage, coarsely chopped
1/4 cup water
3 large potatoes, diced
1 dash seasoning salt
1 dash paprika
2 cups cooked ham, cubed

In a large skillet over medium heat, sauté onions in the margarine. When tender, add cabbage and stir. Pour water over the top, cover, and simmer gently on medium-low for 10 minutes. Stir in potatoes, seasoning salt, and paprika; cover and simmer for 20 more minutes. Mix ham in and finish cooking until ham is hot and potatoes are done (5-10 minutes).

Chicken Kiev

2 tablespoons onion, chopped
2 tablespoons parsley, chopped
3 cloves garlic, chopped
1/4 cup margarine

2 Ener-G egg replacers
1/4 cup flour
1 cup bread crumbs, dried
4 chicken breasts
2 tablespoons margarine or olive oil

In a small bowl, combine onion, parsley, and garlic. Cut a half stick of cold margarine lengthwise into 4 sticks, each measuring 2 ½ inches x ½ inch. On foil, make a pile of bread crumbs and a pile of flour. Have egg replacer right next to it. Place one chicken breast at a time into large zip top bag. Use a meat mallet or heavy saucepan to pound each chicken breast to 1/8 inch thick. Sprinkle each with salt and pepper. Top with onion mixture. Add margarine stick to each chicken breast. Roll chicken breast up. Dip each into flour, then egg replacer, then bread crumbs. Place, seam side down, into a 9 x 13 inches baking pan. Cover and refrigerate for 1-24 hours.

In a large skillet, melt margarine or heat oil. Add chilled chicken rolls. Cook over medium-high for about 5 minutes, turning to brown all sides. Return to baking dish. Bake at 400 °F for 16-20 minutes or until cooked through.

Chicken Cassoulet

4 chicken thighs, bone in and skin on salt and pepper
½ pound bacon, sliced into 1 inch pieces
1 onion, chopped
3 celery stalks, chopped
2 carrots, chopped
4 cloves garlic, chopped
½ cup white wine
1 can (15 ounces) great northern white beans
1 bay leaf
2 teaspoons thyme

½ cup chicken stock
1 tomato, sliced thinly

For Bread Crumbs:
2 tablespoons olive oil
2 cloves garlic, minced
1½ cups fresh bread crumbs salt and pepper to taste

Season chicken with salt and pepper. Let sit at room temperature while you start cooking. In a large skillet, slowly render bacon fat. Remove to a plate when crispy. Add chicken to bacon grease, skin side down. Brown the chicken on both sides then remove to a plate. Add the onion, celery, carrots, and garlic and sauté until soft, about 5 minutes. Deglaze the pan with white wine and reduce by half. Stir in the beans, bay leaf, and thyme. Nestle the chicken thighs and bacon into the pot. Add the chicken stock, cover and bake at 350 °F for 20 minutes.

Meanwhile, prepare garlic bread crumbs. In a small sauté pan, heat oil and stir in garlic until fragrant. Toss in the bread crumbs and cook until golden, about 2-3 minutes. Season with salt and pepper to taste and remove from heat.

Remove chicken from oven, remove the lid, and top with sliced tomatoes and garlic bread crumbs. Return to the oven and bake, uncovered, for 15 more minutes.

Crockpot Meatloaf

1 egg replacer
¼ cup rice milk
2 slices day-old bread, cubed
¼ cup onion, finely chopped
2 tablespoons bell pepper, finely chopped
1 teaspoon salt
¼ teaspoon pepper

RJ Woodward

1½ pounds lean ground meat
¼ cup ketchup
8 medium carrots, cut into 1 inch chunks
8 small red potatoes

In a bowl, combine egg replacer and rice milk. Stir in the bread cubes, onion, bell pepper, salt, and pepper. Add the meat and mix well. Shape into a round loaf. Place in slow cooker. Spread ketchup on top of loaf. Arrange carrots around loaf. Peel a strip around the center of each potato (optional); place potatoes over carrots. Cover and cook on high for 1 hour. Reduce heat to low; cover and cook for 7-8 hours or until meat is cooked and vegetables are tender.

~°~°~°~°~°~°~°~°~°~°~°~°~°~°

"The only way of finding the limits of the possible is by going beyond them into the impossible."
—Arthur C. Clarke

MY SPECIAL RECIPES

Diabetic

"Some people change when they see the light, others when they feel the heat."—Caroline Schoeder

Instant Millionaire Pie

1 (9 inch) prepared graham cracker crust
1 (1 ounce) package sugar-free instant vanilla pudding mix
1 cup cold milk
1 (8 ounces) can crushed pineapple, drained
1 (8 ounces) container frozen whipped topping, thawed
1 cup chopped pecans

In a medium bowl, whisk together pudding mix and milk. Fold in pineapple, whipped topping, and pecans. Pour mixture into prepared crust. Chill at least 2 hours before serving.

Herbed Chuck Steaks

1/3 cup red wine vinegar
1/3 cup water
1 tablespoon olive oil
1 tablespoon chopped fresh thyme
½ teaspoon white sugar salt and pepper to taste
2 pounds beef chuck steaks, well trimmed

In a large bowl, combine the vinegar, water, oil, thyme, sugar and salt and pepper to taste. Add the steaks, mixing well, and let marinate in the refrigerator for 6-8 hours.

Prepare an BBQ grill with an oiled rack set 6 inches from the coals. On a gas grill, set heat to medium.

Remove steaks from the marinade and reserve the marinade. Grill 14-20 minutes for rare, 20 minutes for medium, or 26 minutes for well done, brushing with reserved marinade. Remove from grill and carve into thin slices.

Grilled Caribbean Chicken Breasts

1/4 cup fresh orange juice
1 teaspoon orange zest
1 tablespoon olive oil
1 tablespoon fresh lime juice
1 teaspoon fresh ginger root, minced
2 cloves garlic, minced
¼ teaspoon hot pepper sauce
½ teaspoon fresh oregano, chopped
1½ skinless, boneless chicken breasts

In a food processor, combine the orange juice, orange peel, olive oil, lime juice, ginger, garlic, hot pepper sauce and oregano. Blend into a marinade.

Place chicken breasts in a nonporous glass dish or bowl. Pour marinade over chicken, cover dish or bowl and refrigerate to marinate for at least 2 hours, or up to 24 hours.

Preheat oven to broil or preheat grill to medium high heat and lightly oil grate.

Remove chicken from marinade (disposing of any leftover marinade) and grill or broil 6 inches from the heat source for about 7 minutes per side, or until chicken is cooked through and no longer pink inside.

"Life is a long lesson in humility."
—James M. Barrie

A Surprise-Inside French Toast

6 (2 inch thick) slices French bread
¼ cup ricotta cheese
¼ cup cottage cheese, whipped
2 tablespoons low fat cream cheese
2 teaspoons white sugar
2 teaspoons vanilla
3 cups egg substitute
¼ cup evaporated milk

Cut a pocket in each slice of bread. Open carefully

In a large bowl, combine the ricotta, cottage cheese and cream cheese. Add the sugar and flavouring extract and beat until smooth. Spread the mixture evenly into each bread pocket.

Beat together the egg substitutes and milk. Dip the slices of bread in the egg mixture.

Heat a non-stick pan over medium-high heat. Coat with cooking spray. Cook the toast on each side for about 3-4 minutes per side until golden brown.

Sunday Morning Asian Frittata

1 tablespoon peanut oil
3 green onions, minced
2 teaspoons fresh ginger, grated
2 cloves garlic, minced
1 cup red bell pepper, diced
4 eggs
8 egg whites
2 tablespoons light soy sauce

RJ Woodward

1 cup fresh bean sprouts
1 cup trimmed and halved snow peas
1 tablespoon sesame seeds

Preheat oven to 350 °F (175 °C).

In a large non-stick, oven-proof skillet over medium-high heat, heat the oil. Add the scallions, ginger, and garlic and sauté for 1 to 2 minutes. Add the red pepper and sauté for 3 minutes.

In a medium mixing bowl, mix together the eggs and soy sauce. Add to the skillet. Cook over medium heat for 8-10 minutes until eggs are set on bottom.

Place the bean sprouts and snow peas over the eggs. Sprinkle with sesame seeds. Place in the oven at 350 °F (175 °C) and bake just until top is set, about 8-10 minutes. Watch carefully that eggs are just cooked and do not become tough. Set oven to broil. Broil the frittata for 30 seconds just to give it a nice browned color. Serve in wedges.

Apple Raisin Cakes

2 eggs, beaten
1 cup applesauce
1 teaspoon ground cinnamon
2 teaspoons white sugar
1 cup all-purpose flour
½ cup whole wheat flour
2 teaspoons baking powder
2 teaspoons vanilla
½ cup raisins

In a large mixing bowl, combine eggs, applesauce, cinnamon, sugar, flour, baking powder, vanilla, and raisins. Form small cakes out of the batter.

Heat a non-stick griddle over medium heat, fry the cakes until both sides are browned, about 5-7 minutes.

Pumpkin Spice Muffins

2 cups whole wheat flour
2 teaspoons baking powder
1 teaspoon baking soda
2 teaspoons ground cinnamon
2 teaspoons ground nutmeg
2 eggs, beaten
1 cup pumpkin puree
¼ cup white sugar
2 cups unsweetened applesauce
2 tablespoons vegetable oil
1 teaspoon almond extract

Preheat the oven to 350 °F (175 °C). In a medium bowl, mix together flour, baking powder, baking soda, cinnamon and nutmeg; set aside.

In a large bowl, combine eggs, pumpkin, sugar, applesauce, vegetable oil, and almond extract. Slowly add the flour mixture to the large bowl until just blended. Do not over beat. Pour the batter into 18 non-stick muffin cups.

Bake for 25-30 minutes. Remove muffins from the oven, and let cool slightly. Remove the muffins from the pan, and let cool completely.

Black Bean Spread
1½ cups cooked black beans
3 tablespoons hot salsa
2 green onions, chopped
2 cloves garlic, minced
½ cup low-fat cottage cheese
1 teaspoon hot pepper sauce
2 teaspoons ground cumin
1 teaspoon ground coriander seed salt and pepper to taste

Combine black beans, salsa, green onions, garlic, cottage cheese, hot pepper sauce, cumin, coriander, salt and pepper in an electric blender and blend until smooth. Add a little water, if necessary, to blend mixture thoroughly.

Spinach and Pine Nuts

3 pounds spinach, rinsed
2 teaspoons olive oil
2 tablespoons toasted pine nuts
1 teaspoon minced garlic freshly ground black pepper

Wash the spinach, but allow the water to cling to the leaves. Cook the spinach until it wilts in a skillet over medium-high heat, about 3 minutes.

Heat the oil in a skillet over medium-high heat. Add the spinach, pine nuts, and garlic and cook for 2 minutes. Season with pepper and serve.

Buttermilk Cornbread Muffins

1 cup cornmeal
1 cup all-purpose flour
2 teaspoons baking powder
1 teaspoon baking soda
2 eggs, beaten
¾ cup low fat buttermilk
¼ cup honey
2 tablespoons vegetable oil

Preheat the oven to 375 °F (190 °C).

In a large bowl, combine the cornmeal, flour, baking powder, and soda. Combine eggs, buttermilk, honey, and oil; add slowly to the dry ingredients. Mix until blended. Pour into non-stick muffin cups, making them about 2/3 full.

Bake until golden, about 20-25 minutes. Remove the muffins from the pan and cool completely.

Blueberry Bake

1 cup whole wheat pastry flour
1 teaspoon baking powder
½ teaspoon baking soda
1 tablespoon white sugar
½ cup low fat buttermilk
2 tablespoons honey
1 tablespoon white sugar
1 tablespoon cornstarch
1 teaspoon ground cinnamon
1 cup water
2 tablespoons lemon juice
3 cups fresh blueberries

Preheat oven to 400 °F (200 °C).

To Make Biscuit Topping: In a medium bowl combine flour, baking powder, baking soda, and 1 tablespoon sugar. Mix well then stir in buttermilk just until all ingredients are moistened and dough forms a ball. Set aside.

To Make Berry Filling: In a large saucepan combine honey, 1 tablespoon sugar, cornstarch, cinnamon, water, and lemon juice. Mix until smooth, then add berries. Simmer over medium heat, stirring gently, until thickened (about 10 minutes). Spoon berry mixture into an 8 x 11 inch non-stick casserole dish.

Drop biscuit dough onto berry mixture by tablespoonfuls.

Bake in preheated oven for 20 minutes, or until biscuits are lightly browned.

<u>MY SPECIAL RECIPES</u>

Candy

White Chocolate Eggnog Fudge

2 cups sugar
½ cup butter
¾ cup dairy eggnog
3 (3½ ounces) packages white chocolate, confectionary bars, broken
½ teaspoon nutmeg, grated
1 (7 ounces) jar marshmallow crème
1 teaspoon rum extract

Combine sugar, butter and eggnog in a heavy 2½-3 quart saucepan.

Bring to a full boil, stirring constantly. Continue boiling 8-10 minutes over medium heat or until a candy thermometer reaches 234 °F, stirring constantly to prevent scorching. Remove from heat.

Stir in white chocolate pieces and nutmeg until smooth. Add marshmallow crème nuts and rum extract. Beat until well blended

Pour into buttered 8 or 9 inches square pan.

ᵒ ᵒ ᵒ ᵒ ᵒ ᵒ ᵒ ᵒ ᵒ ᵒ ᵒ ᵒ ᵒ ᵒ ᵒ ᵒ

Turkish Delight Candy

8 tablespoons granulated gelatine
1/2 cup cold water
2 cups sugar
1/2 cup boiling water
1 orange (rind and juice)
3 tablespoons lemon juice nuts or shredded coconut or candied fruit (optional)

Soften gelatine in cold water. Make a syrup of sugar and water; when boiling add gelatine; boil gently 35 minutes. Remove from heat. Add fruit juices; strain. Add candied fruit, nuts or shredded coconut. Pour into a pan moistened with cold water. When firm cut in squares using a knife dipped in hot water. Roll in confectioners' sugar or fruit sugar.

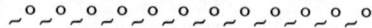

Divinity Candy

3 cups sugar
1 cup corn syrup
¾ cup water
3 egg whites, well-beaten
2 cups walnuts, chopped
1 tablespoon vanilla

Boil first three ingredients until quite brittle in cold water, then pour slowly and gradually into the eggs and beat until it stiffens. Add vanilla and nuts and pour onto a buttered platter. When cold cut in squares.

Tips For Making Divinity Candy

For divinity to harden properly, it's always best to make it on a day that's not too humid. Finish beating the divinity mixture, then work quickly to pour or drop the mixture onto a buttered platter or waxed paper, since it is quick to harden.

Add several drops of water if the divinity mixture becomes too thick. Continue beating if the mixture remains too thin. It is best to store divinity candy in an airtight container until ready for serving.

Sea foam Candy

Easy Sea Foam Candy
3 cups light-brown sugar
1 cup cold water
1½ tablespoons vinegar
Boil to hard ball stage, beat whites of 2 eggs and pour in the candy. Beat quite stiff, add nuts and vanilla.
Old Fashioned Recipe For Sea foam Candy
2 cups brown sugar
1 cup cold water
1 teaspoon of vinegar
1 egg white

Cook sugar and water till it forms a soft ball in water; then add vinegar and pour it on the white of egg, and beat until when dropped from a teaspoon it will form into shape like a bonbon.—Fruit and Candies
Sea Foam Candy Recipe Without Eggs
¾ cup milk
2¼ cups brown sugar
3 tablespoons butter
¾ cup shelled walnuts

Cook milk, butter, and sugar together until it forms a soft ball that will not stick to the fingers in cold water; remove from the fire and add walnuts; beat until it cleaves thick to the spoon; pour on buttered plates.

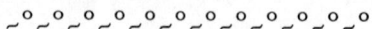

Halloween Taffy

1 cup molasses
1 cup brown sugar
1 tablespoon vinegar
2 teaspoons butter
1 teaspoon baking soda

Mix ingredients and boil until mixture hardens when dropped in cold water, then add teaspoon soda; mix quickly and pour into buttered pans. When cool enough to handle, pull taffy and cut into sticks. Wrap in waxed paper. Put nothing on hands while pulling; keep hands cool. Nutmeats may be stirred into candy just before pouring into pans.

Chewy Chocolate Caramel Candy

3 tablespoons butter
1 cup molasses
¾ cup cream
4 squares unsweetened chocolate
1 cup sugar
½ teaspoon vanilla

Melt butter in a saucepan and add cream, sugar, and molasses. Bring to the boiling-point and add chocolate, balancing it on a large wooden spoon that it may melt gradually with no danger of its burning on the kettle. Continue the boiling, stirring occasionally, until a firm ball may be formed when mixture is tried in cold water, add vanilla, and turn into a buttered pan, having the mixture three-fourths inch in depth.

When nearly cold, cut in cubes, using scissors, or a sharp knife. Wrap in squares of paraffin paper, and let stand in a cold place to harden.

~°~°~°~°~°~°~°~°~°~°~°~°~°

Pull Toffee Candy

Combinations: 3 cups corn syrup or 2 cups corn syrup and 1 cup molasses; or 2 cups corn syrup and 1 cup honey.

Place either syrup combination in a saucepan with 3/4 teaspoon salt. Butter the inside upper edge of the pan to prevent boiling over. Cook until the mixture forms a hard ball, when dropped in cold water. Pour candy mixture into a buttered, shallow pan. Let it stand to cool until it can be handled. When cool, butter the hands and pull. Cut into sticks when done and wrap in waxed paper.

For Vanilla Candies, use white corn syrup, and add 1-1/2 teaspoons vanilla before pouring candy in the pan.

For Peppermint, add a few drops of oil of peppermint while pulling.

For Chocolate, add 3 squares chocolate to syrup.

For Nut Candy, add 3/4 cup chopped nuts to either vanilla or chocolate as it is cooling, fold in toward center as it cools and pull.

~°~°~°~°~°~°~°~°~°~°~°~°~°

Vanilla Caramel Candy

2 cups granulated sugar
½ cup light corn syrup
1 cup sweetened condensed milk
½ cup heavy cream
1 cup milk
¼ cup butter
2 teaspoons vanilla

Mix together all ingredients except vanilla, and cook over a low flame, stirring constantly, until thermometer reads 246ºF. Remove from fire, beat, add vanilla, and turn at once into a slightly greased pan. When cold, remove from pan and cut, using a large sharp knife.

Caramel Making Tips:

Cook over a low flame.

Stir constantly. Caramels burn very easily.

Wrap each caramel in waxed paper immediately.

Homemade Candy Bars

Nut Chocolate Candy Bar
3 egg whites

7 ounces powdered sugar
1½ squares Chocolate
¼ pound almonds

Beat whites of eggs until stiff and add gradually, while beating constantly, powdered sugar. Fold in dark chocolate (which has been melted over hot water then cooled slightly) and three-fourths of the almonds, blanched and chopped.

Spread to one-fourth inch in thickness in a buttered dripping-pan, sprinkle with remaining chopped nutmeats and bake in a very slow oven forty-five minutes.

Cut in finger-shaped pieces or bars and remove from pan. Pile log cabin fashion on a fancy plate for serving.

_o _o _o _o _o _o _o _o _o _o _o _o _o _o _o

Fig Candy Bar
2 envelopes Knox® Gelatine
2 cups cold water
2 cups sugar
1/2 pound figs
¼ cup walnuts, chopped
¼ cup almonds, chopped, blanched
1 orange
1 lemon

Soak gelatine in one cup of the cold water ten minutes. Force figs through a food chopper, add juice of lemon, juice of orange and grated rind of orange, bring to the boiling-point and let simmer ten minutes.

Put sugar and remaining water in saucepan and when sugar is dissolved add soaked gelatine. Bring to the boiling-point and let boil ten minutes; then add fig mixture and boil ten minutes, stirring constantly. Remove from range and add nutmeats.

Pour into shallow pan, first dipped in cold water, and let stand overnight. Cut in pieces two and one-half inches by one-half inch. Roll in powdered sugar.

Fruity French Bars
1 cup figs
1 cup seeded raisins
1 cup dates, pitted
½ cup shredded coconut
2 orange rinds, grated
2 tablespoons lemon juice
1 tablespoon orange juice
½ cup maraschino cherries granulated sugar ground nuts

Put figs, raisins, and dates through food grinder. Combine with the coconut, fruit juices and rind. Blend thoroughly. Work in the cherries, cut into small pieces, being careful not to mash them.

Press into a bar 1 inch square and cut into ½ inch pieces. Roll each piece in granulated sugar, dust them with the ground nuts, and put on waxed paper to dry. This makes about 4 dozen pieces.

Peanut Bar
Slip the skins from enough roasted peanuts to make a cupful. When ready for use, roll them quite fine. Melt two cupfuls of light-brown sugar, and when it bubbles well, stir in the peanuts. Pour at once into buttered pans, and mark into bars before it hardens. No water is required.

Cinnamon Candy Bar
10 ounces almond paste

1 egg, white
5 ounces confectioners' sugar
½ teaspoon cinnamon

Dredge a board with sugar, knead mixture slightly, and shape in a long roll. Pat, and roll one-fourth inch thick, using a rolling pin. After rolling, the piece should be four inches wide. Spread with frosting made of white of one egg and two-thirds cup confectioners' sugar, beaten together until stiff enough to spread. Cut to size.

Work together almond paste and sugar on a smooth board or surface. Then add whites of eggs gradually, and work until mixture is perfectly smooth. Confectioners at first use the hand, afterwards a palette knife, which is not only of use for mixing but for keeping board clean.

<u>MY SPECIAL RECIPES</u>

Children's Fun

Tiny Pizzas

1 standard-sized bagel, cut in half tomato sauce shredded mozzarella cheese toppings like diced green pepper, chopped onion, or chopped tomato (whatever you like) seasonings like oregano, basil, and pepper

Basic Needs: oven (you'll need help from your adult assistant) knife (you'll need help from your adult assistant) baking sheet

Preheat the oven to 325 °F.

Spread tomato sauce on each bagel half. Sprinkle the shredded cheese all over the tomato sauce on each half.

Add your favorite toppings. Put a light sprinkling of seasonings on each half.

Put your bagel halves on the baking sheet.

Bake in the oven on low heat for about 5-8 minutes. You'll know they're done when the cheese is bubbly.

Let cool for a minute, then enjoy your tiny pizzas!

~°~°~°~°~°~°~°~°~°~°~°~°

Disappearing Zucchini Muffins

1½ cups shredded zucchini (about 2 small)
2 cups whole-grain pancake or biscuit mix
1 teaspoon cinnamon
1 teaspoon allspice

RJ Woodward

2 eggs
¾ cup brown sugar
¼ cup unsweetened applesauce
2 teaspoons fresh lemon juice powdered sugar (enough to dust the muffins)

Basic Needs:
oven (you'll need help from an adult assistant) bowls—one large, one medium grater—a plastic grater is safest for kids measuring cups and spoons muffin tin and paper liners

Wash zucchini and remove ends. Shred zucchini using largest holes on grater.

Wrap grated zucchini in a couple of paper towels and squeeze to remove water. Measure 1½ cups of squeezed-dry zucchini.

Preheat oven to 375 °F. Line a 12-cup muffin tin with paper liners.

In a large bowl, mix whole-grain pancake mix (or biscuit mix) with spices.

In a separate bowl, whisk together eggs, brown sugar, applesauce, and lemon juice.

Fold the egg-sugar mixture and shredded zucchini into the pancake-spice mixture; do not over-mix.

Fill each muffin cup 2/3 full with batter.

Bake 10-15 minutes or until golden.

Remove muffins from tin (with help from your adult assistant) and cool on a wire rack.

Sprinkle muffins with a dusting of powdered sugar.

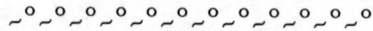

Garden Chicken Wrap

4 whole-wheat wraps (8 inches)
2 cups store-bought rotisserie chicken, shredded
½ cup shredded carrots
1 avocado, thinly sliced
1 cup baby spinach leaves
¼ cup of your favorite fat-free/low-fat dressing (about 1 tablespoon per wrap)

> Basic Needs:
> Cutting board
> Sharp knife
> Measuring cups

Place wraps side by side on a flat surface. Divide chicken into four portions (about ½ cup each). Place a portion of chicken on each wrap.

Top each wrap with carrots, avocado, and spinach. (Have an adult help with the chopping.)

Drizzle dressing evenly over each wrap. Roll each wrap up tightly and cut on the diagonal.

Serve immediately or wrap tightly in aluminum foil and refrigerate for lunch the next day.

Breakfast On The Go

¾ cup fruit-flavoured, fat-free yogurt
1/3 cup oat bran
1/3 cup sliced peaches, canned in light syrup
1 tablespoon dried cranberries

> Basic Needs:
> 16 ounces plastic cup measuring cup measuring spoon

Layer peach slices in plastic cup. Next, layer the yogurt on top of the peach slices.

Sprinkle dried cranberries on top of the yogurt. Top with oat bran.

Serve immediately or cover and refrigerate until ready to eat.

~°~°~°~°~°~°~°~°~°~°~°~°~°

Zesty Turkey Tenderloin

1 pound boneless and skinless turkey breast tenderloin
1½ teaspoons ground cumin
3 garlic cloves, minced
2 tablespoons red wine vinegar
2 teaspoons sugar substitute with sucralose
2 teaspoons cornstarch
1 cup tomatoes, chopped
½ cup zucchini, chopped
½ cup yellow squash, chopped
½ cup onion, chopped
2 tablespoons fresh cilantro, chopped
1 tablespoon jalapeño pepper, chopped (adult assistance needed)

Basic Needs: oven (you'll need help from your adult assistant) knife (you'll need help from your adult assistant) measuring cup measuring spoon broiler pan
3-quart saucepan meat thermometer

Preheat broiler. Combine cumin and garlic in a small bowl and rub mixture on both sides of turkey.

Place turkey on broiler pan and broil for 5 minutes. Turn and broil 5 minutes or until internal temperature reaches 185 °F (85 °C). Juices should run clear and the turkey should not be pink in the center.

While turkey is cooking, combine vinegar, sugar substitute, and cornstarch in saucepan and mix until smooth.

Stir in zucchini, squash, onions, cilantro, and jalapeño peppers.

Cook and stir vegetables over medium heat until mixture boils and thickens. Cook and stir 2 minutes more after mixture begins to thicken.

Spoon over turkey.

Vegetable Skillet Frittata

1½ cups hash browns
1½ cups egg whites
½ cups onion, chopped
½ cups red pepper, chopped
1 cup broccoli florets, cut into small pieces
¾ cup light cheddar cheese
1 tablespoon margarine

Basic Needs:
10" skillet (you'll need help from your adult assistant) measuring cup knife (you'll need help from your adult assistant) aluminum foil

Preheat broiler. Wrap handle of skillet with non-stick aluminum foil.

In skillet, sauté vegetables and hash browns in 1 tablespoon light margarine over medium heat for 5 minutes.

Spread hash browns and vegetables evenly in skillet. Pour egg whites into skillet over the hash browns and vegetables.

Cook until eggs are almost set.

Top with cheese. Broil until cheese is melted.

Chicken With Beans And Rice

16 ounces boneless, skinless chicken breast, cooked and in bite size pieces
2 garlic cloves, minced
¾ cup salsa
1 (15 ounces) can black beans, drained
½ cup red pepper, chopped
½ teaspoon cumin
¼ cup onion, minced
2 tablespoons canned hot chili peppers, minced
2 cups cooked instant rice

Basic Needs:
stove (you'll need help from your adult assistant)

Mix together all ingredients, except rice, in a skillet.
Simmer on top of stove for 10 minutes.
Serve over rice.

~°~°~°~°~°~°~°~°~°~°~°~°~°

Tips
Other Uses for Shampoo
For a stuck zipper, put a drop of shampoo on a Q-tip and dab it onto the zipper. The shampoo will help the zipper to slide easily.

* Buff your shoes. In a pinch, you can revitalize leather shoes and purses by using a small amount of shampoo on a clean cloth. Rub into worn areas as you would shoe polish, and give it a buff. This also offers some protection from salt stains.
* Skip specialty (read: expensive) soaps for hand-washing laundry, use just a drop or two of shampoo instead.

* Shampoo works well on laundry stains-treat the stain with a few drops of shampoo, rub them in, let soak, and then launder as usual.

* Worse than a wound is often the removal of a bandage. Let a few drops of shampoo soak through the adhesive part and the bandage should peel off without pain and sticking.

* In a pinch, shampoo can be used as a substitute for bubble bath.

* Shampoo (conditioner, too) works as a great substitute shaving cream. Lather up, shave away. Shampoo is much more nourishing/less drying than soap, which is what many women use on their legs.

* Harsh soap can dry out hands, but sometimes you need something strong for extra grime-next time, try using shampoo as a hand cleanser. It tackles messes without drying out your skin. You can also just put it in your liquid soap dispenser for everyday use.

* Shampoo works well to remove body oil and gunk from combs and hairbrushes; comb out any loose hair and swish the comb/brush in some warm water and shampoo. Let it soak for a few minutes, then rinse well.

* You can clean houseplant leaves using a few drops of shampoo in a bowl of water; dip a towel in the solution, wring it out, and wipe away dust.

* For a quick touch up cleanse of tub, shower or sink, use some shampoo as a liquid cleaner. It rinses clean and makes chrome shine as well.

* To clean paint brushes use a few drops of shampoo and massage it through the bristles, then rinse well. (Never use extra hot water when washing paint brushes, it loosens the glue resulting in bristle loss!)

* Try shampoo on rug and carpet spills, dab a few drops on with some water and blot with a towel. Repeat until spill is gone.

* A few drops of shampoo rubbed onto the inside surface of a swimming mask (then rinsed) will prevent the mask from fogging up.
* Diluted shampoo can take the place of bubble soap for bubble-blowing wands.
* Car car-washing suds, add ¼ cup shampoo to a pail of warm water and lather up the car as usual.
* Shampoo mixed with baking soda into a paste can be used to clean chrome on vehicles; rinse thoroughly and buff to shine.
* Loosen stuck nuts and bolts with a drop of shampoo. Let it seep into the threads and the bolt should loosen easily.
* Use shampoo to lubricate squeaky hinges.

Use shampoo for oily hair to remove permanent marker

<u>MY SPECIAL RECIPES</u>

<u>Canning and Preserves</u>

TIP:

Do Not use Iodized Salt in making pickles, it causes them to become soft.

Freezer Jam

Freezer jam is easy to make. And because freezer jam isn't cooked, it tastes remarkably like fresh fruit.

There are just a few ingredients:

Fruit Use perfectly ripe fruit. Since you won't be cooking it, the flavour of the jam is going to be much like the flavour of the fruit. If it's over—or under-ripe, you'll be able to taste it. Jam made with under-ripe fruit, besides being sour, might jell too much, while jam made with overripe fruit—besides having an off-flavour and may not jell enough.

Pectin Most recipes call for additional pectin to thicken the jam, giving it that familiar jammy consistency. Commercially produced pectin is derived from fruit—usually apples or citrus. Store-bought pectin comes in two forms: powder and liquid. Most recipes call for powdered pectin, but these are not interchangeable—use whichever form your recipe calls for.

The basic ratios for each packet of powdered pectin are:

3 cups mashed fruit

5 cups sugar, and

1 cup water in which to dissolve and boil the pectin.

This formula can vary a little depending on the brand of pectin, so follow the instructions on the package.

Sugar Sugar inhibits the growth of bacteria, keeping your jam fresh, fruity, and safe to eat. Jam recipes are formulated to call for a certain ratio of pectin to sugar, and they will not jell properly if you don't use the correct amount of sugar. If you'd like to make less-sweet jam, you'll need to buy a special kind of pectin that's formulated to work with less sugar.

Containers

Before you begin making the jam, have all your jam jars ready and waiting. Use either sturdy plastic containers with tight-fitting lids, or short, wide-mouthed glass jars made especially for the freezer.

It's best to choose containers that are no bigger than pint-size; the jam will not set up as well in larger containers. Wash them as you would any other dishes; there's no need to boil them like with traditional jam-making.

Making Jam

The process itself is simple:

Wash and stem the fruit (and peel it, if applicable).

Place it in a wide-bottomed pan and crush with a potato masher to a smooth consistency, leaving some chunks of fruit if you like.

Stir in the sugar and let the mixture sit for 20 minutes, stirring occasionally.

In the meantime, mix together the pectin and water in a small saucepan until the powder is dissolved; bring it to a boil over high heat, and let it boil for a full minute.

Pour it into the fruit and stir for a couple of minutes.

Pour the jam into your containers, leaving a half-inch of "headspace" at the top.

Cover the containers and let them sit at room temperature for 24 hours.

The jam should thicken significantly overnight, but the jelling process can take up to two weeks to complete. If it's too thick, stirring it will soften it up. If it's still too runny after two weeks, pour it into a saucepan and bring it to a boil. It will get thicker as it cools, and you can re-bottle as before.

Storing Your Jam

As the name implies, freezer jam is meant to be stored in the freezer. In fact, it will keep beautifully in the freezer for up to a year. You can also keep freezer jam in the refrigerator for up to three weeks. Once you open a container of jam, you should use it within three weeks as well. Just remember never to keep freezer jam at room temperature, or it will spoil.

Rosy Cider Jelly

3 cups apple cider
1 cup cranberry juice
1 teaspoon lemon juice
1 (1.75 ounces) package powdered fruit pectin
5 cups sugar

In a large saucepan, combine the first four ingredients. Bring to a rolling boil over high heat, stirring constantly. Stir in sugar. Return to a full rolling boil; boil for 1 minute, stirring constantly.

Remove from the heat; skim off any foam. Pour hot liquid into hot jars, leaving ¼ inch headspace. Adjust caps.

Process for 5 minutes in a boiling-water bath

RJ Woodward

Rosemary Jelly

1¼ cups boiling water
2 tablespoons minced fresh rosemary
3 cups sugar
¼ cup vinegar
1 (3 ounces) envelope liquid fruit pectin
2 drops green food coloring

In a large saucepan, combine boiling water and rosemary; cover and let stand for 15 minutes. Strain, reserving liquid. If necessary, add water to measure 1¼ cups. Return liquid to pan; add sugar and vinegar. Bring to a full rolling boil over high heat, stirring constantly. Add pectin, stirring until mixture boils. Boil and stir for 1 minute. Remove from the heat; skim off foam. Add food coloring if desired. Pour hot mixture into hot jars, leaving ¼ inch headspace. Adjust caps. Process for 10 minutes in a boiling-water bath.

~°~°~°~°~°~°~°~°~°~°~°~°~°~°~°

Salsa

10-12 cups of fresh tomatoes cut up that have been blanched and skins peeled*. Squeeze some of the excess juice out as your salsa will become to runny.
4 red peppers
3 green peppers
3 yellow peppers
6 yellow hot peppers
5 jalapeños
5 onions
2-3 heads of garlic
2-3 tablespoons oregano (fresh is best)
2 ½ tablespoons pickling salt

4 tablespoons paprika
¾ cup white vinegar
4 tablespoons cornstarch added to the vinegar
3-4 tablespoons sugar
4 tablespoons ketchup
1 can tomato paste
Yield: 13 pints

*Blanching Tomatoes—Have a large pot of water boiling and another large bowl of cold water nearby. Place about 8-9 tomatoes into the pot of boiling water. Leave for about 1 minute or till tomato skins peel off easy. Take out the tomatoes with a slotted spoon and place into the bowl of cold water. With a paring knife take out the core of the tomato and the take off the skin.

If you are doing a double batch or are short on time you can do the blanching and cutting up of tomatoes and peppers the day before and store them in your refrigerator for the next day. You will need to use some latex gloves when handling your hot peppers as they may burn your skin.

You can experiment with your pepper and garlic amount as you wish. If you like your salsa on the mild side then you may want to cut back on the hot peppers. When tasting your salsa as you are cooking you can put a small amount into a bowl to cool as the peppers are hotter when they are heated. So to get a true taste of what your salsa will taste like you will need to let it cool.

Place all cut up items into a large stock pot. Add the remaining ingredients. Stir all together. Heat up slowly to a low boil and then simmer for 1 hour. Remember to stir often and watch for burning.

While the salsa is cooking you can get your jars washed and sterilize in oven at 225 °F for 10 minutes. Also during the last 20 minutes of cooking your salsa you will want to get the snap lids in a pot of water and boiling for sterilization. You will also need to get some water into your canner and get the water heated up for that.

Fill up your jars leaving a ¾-1 inch space from the top.

Wipe the top of your jars off so there is no salsa to interfere with a proper seal. Place on your snap lids and screw on your rings. Place your filled jars into your already hot water canner. Bring the temperature back up to a boil and boil for 10 minutes. Take out jars and place to cool on a cutting board or whatever else you may have to protect your counter.

Only fill the number of jars that your canner holds with salsa. Keep the rest warm until the first batch comes out of your canner and then fill up more jars with the salsa. Remember when it comes to canning we want to keep our jars, lids and our salsa warm for processing.

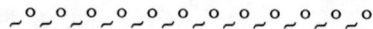

Garlic Jelly

This jelly can be used as a condiment. Add it to meat marinades, brush on roasts or poultry while cooking. Great with crackers and cream cheese

1/4 cup garlic cloves, peeled
2 cups distilled white vinegar
5 cups white sugar
3 ounces liquid pectin

In a food processor or blender, blend the garlic and ½ cup of vinegar until smooth. In a 6-8 quart saucepan, combine the garlic mixture, remaining 1½ cups vinegar and sugar. Over high heat bring the mixture to a boil, stirring constantly. Quickly add the pectin. Return the mixture to a boil and boil hard for 1 minute, stirring constantly. Remove from the heat.

Immediately fill five, sterilized half pint jars with the jelly, leaving ¼ inch head space. Wipe the jar tops and threads clean. Place hot sealing lids on the jars and apply the screw on rings loosely. Process in boiling water in a deep canning pot for 5 minutes. Remove the jars and cool completely. Tighten the jar screw rings to complete the sealing process.

~°~°~°~°~°~°~°~°~°~°~°~°~°~°~°

Garlic Pickles With A Kick

1 (16 ounce) jar dill pickle slices
2 cups white sugar
1 tablespoon hot pepper sauce (e.g. Tabasco™)
6 cloves garlic, peeled
1/4 teaspoon red pepper flakes

Pour the jar of pickles and the liquid into a large bowl. Stir in the sugar, hot pepper sauce, garlic and red pepper. Return to the pickle jar and refrigerate for at least 1 day before serving to soak up the flavors.

~°~°~°~°~°~°~°~°~°~°~°~°~°~°~°

<u>MY SPECIAL RECIPES</u>

<u>PETS</u>

"The difference between friends and pets is that friends we allow into our company, pets we allow into our solitude."—Robert Brault

How To Make Your Own Pet Food Recipes

As a pet owner, no doubt you want to give your dog or cat the best care possible. And caring for your pet means feeding him the best diet you can.

Animals, because they are color blind, choose their foods by smell. Most dogs like gamey flavors best, as well as liver, fat, garlic, horsemeat, lamb, beef, cheese and fish.

Cats enjoy chicken, liver, fish, turkey, lamb, and prefer fresh to aged flavors. Remember that cats are fussy eaters and it is not wise to continually feed them their favorite foods. Soon they will refuse to eat anything else; it is your job to see your cat has a balanced diet.

Warning: Do not feed cats onions!

Animals do not need salt added to their diet as the natural salt in the food is enough for them.

Dogs may eat any vegetable they want, but cats should not have any starchy veggies, like peas and corn. Some dogs and cats even enjoy fruits!

It's a good idea to always add a grain, such as Kibble, wheat germ, cooked oatmeal or whole wheat bread to meat dinners. For dogs use 75% carbohydrate foods (grains and vegetables) to 25% meat.

You will find, once you begin making your own pet foods, that it is really relatively simple and you will save some money as well. remember that all pet foods should be served at room temperature; don't serve food cold from the refrigerator nor hot from the stove.

Incidentally, you should know that cats should be fed three times a day, while an adult dog needs only one meal a day.

Cats are healthier on a diet of raw meat supplemented with priobiotics. Consult with your veterinarian before offering a raw meat diet to an immune-compromised cat. Meat should be fresh and frozen for 24 hours then thawed and offered to your cat. Consult your veterinarian before suddenly changing the diet. Many pet stores offer raw foods in the cooler section.

One site states "Some raw food proponents also add other ingredients:

- o fresh, raw vegetables, including broccoli, carrots, squash, and potatoes
- o raw fruits (apples, cranberries, and bananas are frequently mentioned)
- o grain, such as barley, oats, or brown rice (whole, ground, or sprouted)"

Here are some cooked pet recipes you can make at home. Limit the amount of liver that you pet eats.

* **<u>SAUTEED LIVER</u>**

- o Heat 1 teaspoon corn oil in a pan.
- o Add 1/4 pound beef liver and fry on both sides until cooked but not dry inside.
- o Add 1/2 cup water to the pan and mix it up with all the brown bits.
- o For dogs, cut the liver into pieces and serve; for cats, grind the liver in a blender, using the pan juices.

* **VEAL STEW**

   o Combine 1/2 pound stewing veal, 1 cup canned tomatoes, 1 cup water, 1 chicken bouillon cube, and parsley in a pot and simmer.
   o When meat is tender, remove all the bones.
   o For dogs, cut the meat in chunks, and mix stew with kibble or some other grain; for cats, grind the stew in blender, adding a tablespoon of wheat germ.

* **CHICKEN SOUP**

   o Combine 1 chicken liver, 1 giblet, 1 chicken heart, 1 chicken neck, 2 cups water and 1 tablespoon finely chopped parsley.
   o Cover and simmer until the giblet is tender.
   o Chop all the meat for dogs removing bones and mix with kibble; for cats, you may want to grind the meat in the blender.

* **LIVER COOKIES**

   o Preheat oven to 350 °F.
   o Combine 1/2 cup dry milk and 1/2 cup wheat germ; drizzle 1 teaspoon honey on top.
   o Add one 3 oz. cooked blended liver and stir until everything is well mixed.
   o Form the mixture into balls; place them on an oiled cookie sheet and flatten them with a fork.
   o Bake 8 to 10 minutes.
   o Consistency should be fudgy.
   o Store in a jar in the fridge; freeze if keeping more than a few days.

❉ **MACKEREL DINNER**

o   Heat 1 tsp. corn oil in a skillet and fry 1 small mackerel until it flakes apart easily. Remove and cool. Pour 1/2 cup hot water into the pan and scrape the brown bits into it. Remove the bones from the fish and mix with the juice. For dogs, serve in pieces with kibble; for cats, grind with the pan juices.

❉ **BEEF COOKIES**

o   Following the recipe for Liver Cookies, using cooked beef puree instead.

❉ **FISH COOKIES**

o   Follow the recipe for Liver Cookies but use instead 3 1/2 ounces of mashed and boned mackerel, either canned or freshly cooked.

❉ **DOG MORSELS**

o   2 cups whole wheat flour
o   2 tsp. garlic powder
o   2 cups white flour
o   1 cup skim milk powder
o   2 eggs water
o   1/2 cup melted beef or pork drippings (or lard)
o   Preheat oven to 350 °F. Mix ingredients together with enough water to make a stiff dough. Roll out and cut into Christmas shapes. Bake on cookie sheet until hard.

❉ **BUDGIE BROWNIES**

o   1 cup cornmeal
o   1 tsp. finely ground cuttlebone

- o 1 cup hulled millet
- o 2 tbsp. liquid honey
- o 1/4 cup whole wheat flour
- o 2 eggs
- o 2 tbsp. raw wheat germ
- o 4 egg yolks (for larger birds add 1/2 cup peanuts)
- o Preheat oven to 350 °F. Place all ingredients into a bowl and mix well. Pat into a greased and floured baking dish.
- o Bake for 30 minutes or until firm (if edges start to get too brown, cover with foil).
- o Cool and cut into small squares.

Pooch Recuperation Food
If ever your pet is feeling a little under the weather, I recommend this."
4 cups low-salt chicken broth
2 cups rice
1 (15 ounce) can cut green beans, drained

In a saucepan bring chicken broth to a boil. Add rice and stir. Reduce heat, cover and simmer for 20 minutes. Once rice has cooked, stir in drained green beans.

Cool to room temperature before serving; refrigerate leftovers.

> *"Animals are such agreeable friends—they ask no questions, they pass no criticisms."*
> —*George Eliot*

Doggie Treats
1 cup all-purpose flour
1 cup corn flour
1 cup cornmeal
½ cup smooth peanut butter
1 cup water

1/3 cup vegetable oil
1 egg

Preheat oven to 375 °F (190 °C). Whisk together the flour, corn flour, and cornmeal in a mixing bowl. Lightly grease two baking sheets.

Place the peanut butter in a microwave safe dish, and cook in the microwave a few seconds at a time until the peanut butter has liquefied. Stir the peanut butter, water, vegetable oil, and egg into the flour mixture until a stiff dough forms. Roll out on a floured surface and cut into treat shapes with a cookie cutter. Place the treats onto the prepared cookie sheets.

Bake in the preheated oven until golden, 10-12 minutes. Allow the treats to cool on the baking sheets for 5 minutes before removing to a wire rack to cool completely. Store in an airtight container.

Gourmet Dog Biscuits
3 cups all-purpose flour
3 cups whole wheat flour
2 cups cracked wheat
1 cup cornmeal
1 tablespoon garlic powder
1 tablespoon brewers' yeast
1/2 cup dry milk powder
3 cups beef broth
1/8 cup milk

Preheat oven to 300 °F (150 °C). Grease a cookie sheet.

In a large mixing bowl combine white flour, whole wheat flour, cracked wheat, cornmeal, garlic powder, brewer's yeast and instant milk. Stir in 2 cups broth. Mix the ingredients well using either your hands or an heavy duty electric mixer. The dough should be very stiff. Gradually mix in the remaining 1 cup broth to make a bread-dough consistency.

Roll the dough out to a 1/4 inch to 1/2 inch thickness on a floured board. Cut out biscuits into any shape you please. Place the biscuits on the prepared cookie sheet. Brush the tops of the biscuits lightly with milk.

Bake the cookies 45 minutes; turn oven off completely but do not remove the biscuits. Let the biscuits sit in the oven overnight (for 10 hours). Store biscuits in an air-tight container.

Kitty Kisses
1 (3 ounces) can wet cat food
1 teaspoon catnip (optional)

Preheat an oven to 350 °F (175 °C). Line a baking sheet with foil or parchment paper.

Place the cat food and catnip into a blender. Cover, and puree until smooth and looks a little like frosting. Spoon pureed cat food into a resealable plastic bag. Cut a small hole in the corner of the bag.

Squeeze ½ inch kisses onto the prepared baking sheets. Bake 15 minutes. Cool completely and store in an airtight container

> *"Man is rated the highest animal, at least among all animals who returned the questionnaire."*—Robert Brault

Flea Terminator Dog Treats
3 cubes beef bouillon
1 ½ cups boiling water
2 cups whole wheat flour
1 cup cornmeal
2/3 cup brewers' yeast
2 tablespoons garlic powder
2 egg yolks

Preheat the oven to 375 °F (190 °C). Dissolve beef bouillon cubes in boiling water, and set aside. Grease cookie sheets.

In a large bowl, stir together the whole wheat flour, corn meal, brewers' yeast, and garlic powder. Add the yolks, then gradually pour in the bouillon water while stirring. Mix thoroughly to form a firm dough. On a floured surface, roll the dough out to ¼ inch thickness. Cut into desired shapes using cookie cutters. Place cookies one inch apart onto cookie sheets.

Bake for 20 minutes in the preheated oven, then turn the oven off, and leave the cookies inside for at least 3 hours or overnight to harden. Store in an airtight container at room temperature.

<u>*Diabetic Dog Treats*</u>
½ cup whole wheat flour
2 eggs
1 ½ pounds beef liver, cut into pieces

Preheat the oven to 350 °F (175 °C). Line a 10 x 15 inch jellyroll pan with parchment paper.

Place the liver into a food processor. Pulse until finely chopped. If you have room, add the flour and eggs, and process until smooth. Otherwise, transfer to a bowl, and stir in the flour and eggs using a wooden spoon. Spread evenly in the prepared pan.

Bake for 15 minutes in the preheated oven, or until the center is firm. Cool, and cut into squares using a pizza cutter. The treats will have a consistency similar to a sponge. Store in a sealed container in the refrigerator.

Horses

"The kind man feeds his beast before sitting down to dinner."
—*Hebrew Proverb*

Spoil your horse with tried and true tasty recipes.

Apples and carrots are the classic horse treats but you might find your horse is a willing convert when you offer up some of these homemade cookies and other goodies straight from the kitchen to the barn!

Remember if you are introducing a new horse treat recipe or grain to your horse, start gradually with small amounts until your horse becomes accustomed to it.

Hot and Nutritious Horse Treats

You can substitute your current feed for the primary ingredients in these recipes, if you desire.

Here is an excellent horse treat recipe to warm up your equine companion on a blustery day

❋ *Hot Mash*

1 ¾ cups mixed grain (such as a corn, oats, and barley blend)
1 ½ cups flour
¾ cup unsweetened applesauce
2/3 cup dark brown sugar, packed
3 tablespoons dark corn syrup egg white from 1 large egg (well beaten)

Preheat oven to 375 °F. Combine the grain and flour in a bowl and mix thoroughly. In a second, larger bowl, combine applesauce, brown sugar and corn syrup. Stir in egg white and then the dry mixture. Combine well. Drop by spoonfuls onto ungreased cookie sheets, leaving 2 inches of space between each. Bake for 12-14 minutes, until dark brown. Remove to a wire rack and cool. Yield about 25 cookies.

❋ *Steamed Oat Mash*

One of our horse's favourites served up on a cold winter morning! 1 or 2 tablespoon salt. A ration of rolled, crushed or crimped oats. A few cut up carrots. A few cut up apples, 1 cup molasses or 2 tablespoons linseed meal for extra taste. Mix all ingredients in a feed bucket. Combine with suitable quantity of boiling water (completely soaked up by oats). Cover and let steam until cool enough to feed to your horse. (30-45 minutes preparation time)Variation: Use applesauce instead of apples and carrots.

* *Bran Mash*

This horse treat recipe is especially good for pregnant mares during the late months of their term!

8—12 cups wheat bran, 1 cup rolled, crushed or crimped oats ¼ cup corn oil, ¼ cup molasses, 1 ½—2 ½ cups boiling water, 1 carrot, sliced1 apple, sliced. Combine bran and oats in feed bucket. Add boiling water to desired consistency. Stir in oil, molasses, carrot and apple. Cover and allow to sit. Serve when cool enough to feed.

"If all the beasts were gone, men would die from a great loneliness of spirit, for whatever happens to the beasts also happens to the man. All things are connected. Whatever befalls the Earth befalls the sons of the Earth."—Chief Seattle of the Suquamish Tribe, letter to President Franklin Pierce

WILD BIRDS

A few favorite homemade wild bird food recipes.
Sweet Cherry Treat
2 cups of rendered suet
1½ cups of chunky peanut butter
1 cup of dried cherries
1 cup of sunflower seed hearts
1 cup of crushed graham crackers
1½ cups of oatmeal

In a large bowl, add the chunky peanut butter to the rendered suet while it is still warm. Once the peanut butter is melted, add the cherries and the sunflower seed hearts. Then stir in the crushed graham crackers and oatmeal. After all of the ingredients are thoroughly mixed, put the mixture into moulds or on a cookie sheet to cool.

Berries Berries Berries
3 cups of rendered suet
1 ½ cups of chunky peanut butter
1 cup of mixed, dried berries. Strawberries, blueberries, cherries and cranberries.
1 cup of sunflower seed hearts
1 cup of oatmeal
½ cup of corn muffin mix.

In a large bowl, add the chunky peanut butter to the rendered suet while it is still warm. Once the peanut butter is melted, add the dried berries and the sunflower seed hearts. Then stir in the oatmeal and corn muffin mix. After all of the ingredients are thoroughly mixed, put the mixture into moulds or on a cookie sheet to cool.

Hummingbird feeder recipe:
1 part sugar
4 parts water

First, bring the water to a boil and then slowly add the sugar. Let it boil for a few minutes, then remove from the burner to cool. Store any excess nectar in the refrigerator. Yes, it is that easy!

> *"A bird does not sing because it has an answer. It sings because it has a song."*
> Chinese Proverb

RJ Woodward

Wild Bird Shish kabob
Ingredients: apples, oranges, pears, grapes, prunes, dried fruit, berries, summer squash or any other fresh fruits that you have around your kitchen or garden.

Slice the larger items into manageable sizes and poke a hole in the center of each piece. Then tie a large knot in one end of a 3 to 4 foot piece of twine. Run the twine through your fruits and vegetables. Then simply hang your stringed treats over a tree branch and watch as your feathered friends feast on your new offering.

September Harvest
September means apples. There are also many other fruits available. Many migratory birds that eat fruit will be tempted to linger at your feeders if you offer the following mix. Use a platform style feeder when offering this wild bird food mix.
2 cups of dried, chopped apples (dried apples will not get moldy as fast)
2 cups of raisins
2 cups of chopped nuts (almonds, walnuts, or any nuts you have available)
1 cup of chopped prunes
1 cup of dried melon or squash seeds

Simply mix the ingredients together in a large bowl or bucket. Start by adding small amounts to your feeder and store the rest in a paper bag in a cool and dry location. Now your homemade wild bird food is ready to serve.

Peanut Butter Cakes
Wild Birds love peanut butter and suet. This recipe combines both. These birds treats are easy to make and a great project for kids.

1 cup of rendered suet
1 cup of chunky peanut butter
6 cups of cornmeal
1 muffin tin with paper liners

Here is the process for rendering suet: Put the suet into a pan and turn on low heat (overheated fat can catch fire). If possible use an electric skillet. If you are using your stovetop it is best to use an oversized pan.

After the suet melts, pour it through fine cheesecloth into a heatproof container. Then discard the pieces that did not melt. Allow the melted suet to re-harden, either in the fridge or on the counter top. The suet needs to be melted and hardened 2-3 times before it is ready to use. If you do not do this, the suet will not cake properly.

While the suet is still warm, add the chunky peanut butter and stir until melted. Then stir in the cornmeal.

Spoon the mixture into the paper-lined muffin tins. Allow them to cool at room temperature or place them in the refrigerator. They can even be frozen until needed.

You can add any combination of sunflower seeds, raisins, chopped fruit or nuts to spice up your mixture of homemade wild bird food.

Mixed Seeds and Molasses Cornbread Muffins
2 cups self-rising corn meal mix
1 egg (preferably natural vegetarian fed hen eggs)
¼ cup shortening or canola oil
½-2/3 cup milk
1 packet flaxseed
½ cup sesame seeds

1/2 cup molasses(preferably use only pure homemade cane molasses, Dutch Kettle brand, which uses no chemical processing)

Preheat oven to 400 °F

Container needed : 12 cup muffin tin

Mix corn meal, flaxseed, and sesame seeds, add egg, shortening or oil and molasses, then slowly add milk until batter is of thick consistency, spoon batter into muffin tin cups, filling each cup 2/3 full. Bake until golden brown. Remove from muffin tin while warm, let cool completely on rack, then crumble muffins and spread out on a flat outside container or put whole muffins outside for birds to nibble on.

A Special
Melt 3 blocks of lard in a pot then add
1 Jug of ground peanuts
1 jug of thistle seed
1 jug of bird seed
1 small bag of meal worm mix well then pour into baking trays place in fridge over night in the morning cut into blocks. the birds can't get enough of it

Nutty Bird
nuts bread torn into tiny pieces plate
Optional broken up crackers

Put all the stuff onto a plate and mix them around. Place it under a tree or put holes in it and hang it on a tree.

Bird Suet
1 cup of lard
1 cup of peanut butter
1 cup of cornmeal

1 cup of rolled oats
1 cup of wild birdseed

Cream the lard and peanut butter together. Add the other ingredients and mix well. Apply to pine cone or to a wooden bird feeder.

The birds absolutely love it . . . . They sit waiting for us to fill the feeder every day.

Leftover Baked Oatmeal Scramble
½ Stick butter, melted
½ cup brown sugar
1½ teaspoon vanilla
1½ teaspoons cinnamon
3 teaspoons baking powder
1 teaspoon salt
5 cups oatmeal
3 cups water or milk
Mix well. Bake 325 °F for 20 minutes.
Let cool, mix in chopped apple or other dried fruit
Leftover chopped bacon.
Refrigerate. Sprinkle on platform feeder.

Bird Pudding
Melt one cup lard and one cup crunchy peanut butter together.

To this melted mixture add one cup of quick oats, one cup of all purpose flour, 2 cups of yellow corn meal. Mix thoroughly. You may also add 1/2 cup of bird seed and/or raisins to this. This will have the consistency of thick pudding.
Pour mixture into a pan and place it in the refrigerator or freezer and allow to harden.

RJ Woodward

Once mixture has hardened cut or break into pieces to fit into suet baskets. Any crumbles or small pieces can be placed in a platform feeder. Any leftovers may be stored in plastic zip bags and stored in the freezer.

The birds just love this in the winter months . . .

<u>*Super Suet*</u>
Ingredients needed: Lard or Veggie Shortening, whole wheat flour, cornmeal, oats, birdseed, etc.

This recipe is fun to make and birds love it!
1. Put as much lard as you want into a large bowl. (start with about a cup)
2. In a small bowl, mix even amounts of flour and cornmeal.
3. Add the flour/cornmeal mix to the lard and mix it together with your fingers. (wear plastic gloves, it gets greasy!)
4. The lard dough should be non-sticky enough to be able to roll into a ball, if still too sticky, add more flour until it's just right. or if it is not sticky enough, add more lard.
5. Pour the birdseed, oats, or whatever you want into the large bowl and mix it up with the lard dough.
6. Make the dough into a ball again and smoosh it with your hand until it fits into your suet feeder.

Voila! Place in suet feeder and, if you want, stick a stick into the suet to help the less graceful birds get a bite.

<u>*Bird pancakes*</u>
This is fun to make! And it does not use to many ingredients!

1 part shortening
1 part whole wheat flour
½ part of rolled oats

A few yummy things to add in (Bird seed, dried fruit, etc)

1. Put shortening in a bowl and add some of the flour.

2. Mix the flour and e together using your fingers and keep adding the flour until it's all gone.

3. Add the Oats and finger mix it again.

4. Add in the yummy stuff and mix again.

5. Roll mixture into a few balls and flatten with the palms of your hands.

6. If you want, press some yummy stuff on top of the pancake as a topping.

7. Place outside on a plate, window sill, or even on a platform feeder.

8. Watch for the birds to come flocking!

Peanut Butter On A Stick
Birds love this treat. In winter is when they love it the most.

A good size stick, break off the sticks that are on it.
Peanut butter smooth or chunky it doesn't matter.
Bird seed and or peanuts, raisins, fruit, etc.
String to tie on the stick.
Knife to put on the peanut butter.

After you have everything put the string on, hang it up somewhere. Then spread the peanut butter on the stick, make sure there are spaces on the stick so the bird can perch without getting peanut butter on their feathers. Get your seed and other things you want to put on it and put it in your hand and put it on the peanut butter. When you are done hang it up outside and watch as birds enjoy the treat you made for them.

In winter you might have to make it every day if birds love it in your area.

Quick and Easy Apple Dough Suet

Start with a cake of Home-Style Suet.

Kneed it back into a dough.

Add ¼ cup of dried apples.

Place ½ back into the plastic tray. Carefully pop it back out onto a dish. Repeat this with the other 1/2. Refrigerate for 1 hour to make firm.

Fruit Frenzy

Apples, oranges, pear, grapes any fruit that you have at home chop them into small pieces and put into your bird feeder

Find a large pine cone.

Tie a three to four foot piece of yarn around the top of the pine cone for the hanger.

Mix 2 tablespoons of peanut butter with 2 tablespoons of margarine.

Spread the peanut butter and margarine mixture onto the pine cone.

Pour some bird seed onto a plate or shallow dish and roll the pine cone in it.

Place the seed-covered pine cones in the freezer for about an hour or until it is firm.

Hang it outside in a tree!

Tips:
1. Hang your pine cone at the end of a smaller branch so squirrels don't get it.
2. Work with the bird seed over newspaper to help make clean up time easier.

3. Plain peanut butter works well

Christmas Pudding for the Birds
1½ cups melted fat. (Use bacon or beef fat, NO CHICKEN FAT)
2 tablespoons of peanut butter
1½ cups bread crumbs
1 cup oatmeal
½ cup white flour
½ cup cornmeal
¼ cup sugar
½ cup bird seed, raisins etc

Melt fat and peanut butter and stir in other ingredients. Empty the mixture into a pie tin, coffee can or ice cream container. Allow it to cool and harden.

Triple this recipe to make 5½ pints.

Raisin Suet Cubes
1 cup oatmeal
1 cup raisins
1 cup cornmeal
½ cup meat grease
½ cup peanut butter

Mix dry ingredients. Melt grease and peanut butter in microwave. Add to dry ingredients. Mix well. Freeze in ice cubes trays until firm.

Backyard Pinecone Bird Feeder
1 cup softened peanut butter
½ cup graham cracker crumbs
¼ cup black oil sunflowers
¼ cup millet or small seeds, ¼ cup raw oatmeal

¼ cup chopped peanuts (optional if using crunchy peanut butter)
1 whole apple, chopped

Mix together well. Tie twine or strong string to a few large pine or fir cones. Leave enough string or twine to tie to tree branch or other structure. Smear mixer into the crevices of the cones. Use remainder on outside of cones. Hang on a safe limb or branch and enjoy the backyard bird show!

Eggshell Suet for Bluebirds
1 cup lard
1 cup chunky peanut butter
2 cups rolled oats
2 cups yellow cornmeal
1 cup flour
1/3 cup sugar
2/3 cup chicken scratch
1/3 cup washed, dried and crushed eggshells

Melt lard over low heat, Add peanut butter. Stir until melted. Add other ingredients and mix well.

I reuse store bought suet pans. Or you can line a baking pan with wax paper. Spread into pan and cut into squares.

Freeze for about one hour. Remove cakes and store in baggies in the freezer. Not need to that before serving.

Chicken scratch comes in 50 lb bags—I find the cracked corn works. This year I have two bluebird couples coming to eat. But lots of other birds like this too.

Juicy Blast
2 peeled sliced oranges vine of grapes
1 sliced apple kiwi (optional)
3 strawberries something to crush and mix with

Put the peeled sliced oranges in a bowl. If you used kiwi crush it up and put it in the bowl. Take the skin off the apple and cut the apple. Smash 2 out of the three strawberries. Put the third one in the bowl whole. Take the grapes off the vines. Crush them if you want to. Put all the fruits in the same bowl and mix them together. Mix for 2-3 minutes, after that you done.

Easy Peanut Butter Snacks
1 cup peanut butter
½ cup Crisco
½ cup bird seed

Melt peanut butter and Crisco together and mix. Then stir in bird seed. Before it hardens put in a muffin tin liner. Once it hardens put in your feeder.

Goo Cakes
Melt bag of miniature marshmallows, cup of lard, and small jar of chunky peanut butter over low heat. Stir in about 3 cups black oil sunflowers, and after thoroughly coating the seeds, add another 3 cups, plus fruit or nuts if desired. Press into moulds and put in freezer for a couple of hours until they set firmly.

Attracts many types of birds!

We have red-bellied woodpeckers, downy woodpeckers, nuthatches, brown creeper, ruby-crowned kinglets, chickadees, cardinals, pine siskens and many other birds visiting this feeder just outside the window.

Textured Bird Trail Mix
This is a really simple, healthy if not "outside the box" treat for wild birds, not to mention very economical!

I pour this into my stake and bowl feeders in addition to using traditional seed mixes in my tube feeders, and the birds (and squirrels) usually eat the entire mixture within the day!

Whole Oats (not the "instant" type) or Multi-Grain Hot Cereal mixture. Example: rye/barley/oats/wheat

NOTES: one can purchase these very inexpensively at the local grocery store; usually sold in canisters.

Raw, Shelled Sunflower Seeds

Corn Meal

Dried Fruit (i.e. raisins, apricot, pineapple, cranberries)

Simply use a food processor or coffee-bean grinder to lightly grind the seeds and grains, basically cracking some seeds/grains remaining intact for texture. A light grind is best; grind the seeds for 2 seconds, and the grain for the same amount of time, separately.

Put together in a storage container.

Add corn meal.

Chop dried food to bird bite-sized pieces and add to the mix.

Ideally, the mix should have a high-fat ratio (i.e. sunflower seeds) and whole grains for a delicious, filling mix. Keep fresh water nearby at all times. The grains are filling and it's a dry mix.

> *"The very idea of a bird is a symbol and a*
> *suggestion to the poet.*
> *A bird seems to be at the top of the scale, so*
> *vehement and*
> *intense his life . . . . The beautiful vagabonds,*
> *endowed with*
> *every grace, masters of all climes, and knowing*
> *no bounds—how*
> *many human aspirations are realised in their*
> *free, holiday-lives*
> *—and how many suggestions to the poet in their*
> *flight and song!"*
> *John Burroughs*

<u>MY SPECIAL RECIPES</u>

Food Measuring Equivalents

1 pinch = approx 1/8 teaspoon
½ tablespoon = 1 ½ teaspoons
3 teaspoons = 1 tablespoon
¼ cup = 4 tablespoons
1/3 cup = 5 tablespoons + 1 teaspoon
3/8 cup = 6 tablespoons
½ cup = 8 tablespoons
2/3 cup = 10 tablespoons + 2 teaspoons
¾ cup = 12 tablespoons
1 cup =16 tablespoons
4 cups = 1 quart
8 quarts = 1 peck
4 pecks = 1 bushel

Liquid Measures

1 dash = approx a few drops
1 tablespoon = 3 teaspoons
1 tablespoon = ½ fluid ounce
1 fluid ounce = 2 tablespoons
1 jigger = 3 tablespoons or 1 ½ fluid ounces
¼ cup = 4 tablespoons or 2 fluid ounces
½ cup = 8 tablespoons or 4 fluid ounces
1 cup = 16 tablespoons or 8 fluid ounces
1 pint = 2 cups or 16 fluid ounces
1 quart = 2 pints or 32 fluid ounces
1 gallon = 4 quarts or 64 fluid ounces

Temperature Equivalents

Degrees Fahrenheit = Degrees Celsius

Room Temperature	70	21
Luke warm	90	32
Water's Boiling Point	212	100
Low or Cool Oven	250	120
Slow Oven	300	150
Moderately Slow Oven	325	165
Moderate Oven	350	180
Moderately Hot Oven	375	190
Hot Oven	400	205
Very Hot Oven	450-500	230-260
Broil	550	290

Metric Equivalents

Ounces = Grams

1	128
2	57
3	85
4	113
5	142
6	170
7	198
8	227
9	255
10	284
11	312
12	340
13	368
14	397
15	425
16	454

Grams = Ounces

1	.035
50	1.75
100	3.5
250	8.75
500	17.5
750	26.25
1000 (1 kilogram)	35 (2.21 lbs)

Pounds = Kilograms

1	.45
2	.91
3	1.4
4	1.8
5	2.3
6	2.7
7	3.2
8	3.5
9	4.1
10	4.5

Kilograms = Pounds

1	2.2
2	4.4
3	6.6
4	8.8
5	11

"An empty belly is the best cook."
—Estonian Proverb

My Special Recipes

CPSIA information can be obtained at www.ICGtesting.com
Printed in the USA
239335LV00001B/3/P